"As data continue to drive decision making, funding, and policy cultural managers need resources like this book to aid them in learning, doing, and using research."

Constance DeVereaux, *State University of New York at Buffalo, USA*

"Written by five experienced arts management professors, this comprehensive and digestible book about research methods and publication practices in arts and cultural management, specifically, is a much-needed practical resource for undergraduate and graduate students, as well as their professors and mentors. The authors provide clear definitions, detailed research design descriptions and examples that will inspire fellow researchers and professional managers working in an increasingly complex and complicated arts and cultural economy."

Diane Claussen, *DePaul University, USA*

Doing (and Using) Research in Arts and Cultural Management

This book offers a rich, critical, and engaging exploration of cutting-edge methods for studying arts and cultural management in a digital age. The content will appeal to those who seek to study these topics by employing the latest data gathering and analytical methods. It is an informative resource for academics, including advanced masters' and PhD candidates, as well as professional arts managers seeking to understand the changing landscape. This book is relevant to arts and cultural management, creative industries, cultural policy, festivals and events, heritage, museum studies, arts consumption and marketing, and cultural tourism. It will also appeal to consultants, evaluators, and fundraisers who do research on a regular basis. The chapters engage with both traditional and contemporary research topics, including providing examples of high-quality research from national, regional, and local settings in various parts of the world. The co-authors are five diverse scholars who are experienced not only in standard qualitative and quantitative methods but also emerging techniques such as netnography and digital analysis. This book provides real-world, empirical, and theoretical insights on how to navigate the complexities of research methods in a creative context.

François Colbert has been active in the field of arts and culture for over 50 years, particularly in the performing arts, museum, and film sectors. He has given numerous training and professional development seminars in arts management, with a focus on the field of marketing management in a cultural context. He is a professor of marketing and holder of the Carmelle and Rémi Marcoux Chair in Arts Management at HEC Montréal. He founded the AIMAC Conference and the International Journal of Arts Management. He is the codirector of the Master of Management in

International Arts Management and author of the book *Marketing Culture and the Arts*, published in 16 languages.

Jennifer Wiggins is Professor of Marketing and Entrepreneurship at Kent State University, Ohio, USA, and Co-Editor in Chief of the International Journal of Arts Management. Her research on consumer willingness to donate, willingness to pay for arts experiences, and willingness to support new creative and social ventures has been published in top journals in marketing, entrepreneurship, and arts management. Her methodological expertise is in experimental design and measurement. She has mentored over two dozen doctoral students and teaches philosophy of science, theory development, and research methods at the doctoral level.

Russell Belk is York University Distinguished Research Professor and Kraft Foods Canada Chair in Marketing at Schulich School of Business, York University. His research involves the extended self, the arts, collecting, gift-giving, sharing, digital consumption, and materialism. He is primarily qualitative and often conceptual, visual, and cultural. He has over 800 publications; in 2012 a 10-volume subset was published in Sage's Legends in Consumer Behavior series. In 2023 he received an honorary doctorate with festschrift from Université de Reims. He co-initiated the Consumer Behavior Odyssey, the ACR Film Festival, and the Consumer Culture Theory Conference.

Ruth Rentschler OAM is Professor of Arts and Cultural Leadership, UniSA Business, Adelaide, Australia. Her research entails creative topics focusing on inclusion and diversity. Ruth's work is often qualitative, with particular interest in unique longitudinal secondary data sets, the self and others, and more recently film and the digital world. She has designed and taught research methods at the PhD level in numerous universities around the world. Ruth has received national and international awards for her contributions to arts and cultural management and higher education. She is widely published, including her most recent book, *Routledge Companion to Governance in the Arts World* (Rentschler, Reid & Donelli, Routledge, Eds., 2025).

Danilo C. Dantas is Professor of Marketing at HEC Montréal, Canada, where he serves as the pedagogical director of the Professional Master's and Graduate Diploma in Management of Cultural Organizations. His research focuses on the marketing of music, employing various research methods. His work has been published in the *European Journal of Marketing*, the *Journal of Interactive Marketing*, the *International Journal of Arts Management*, and the *Journal of Public Policy & Marketing*, among others. He is also the co-chair of AIMAC, the International Association of Arts and Culture Management.

Discovering the Creative Industries
Series Editor: Ruth Rentschler

The creative and cultural industries account for a significant share of the global economy. Gaining and maintaining employment and work in this sector is a challenge and chances of success are enhanced by ongoing professional development.

This series provides a range of relatively short, student-centred books which blend industry and educational expertise with cultural sector practice. Books in the series provide applied introductions to the core elements of the creative industries. In sum, the series provides essential reading for those studying to enter the creative industries as well as those seeking to enhance their career via executive education.

Entrepreneurship in the Arts, 3e
Bonita M. Kolb

Human Resources in the Arts
Brea M. Heidelberg

Marketing Strategy for the Arts, 3e
Bonita M. Kolb

Doing (and Using) Research in Arts and Cultural Management
François Colbert, Jennifer Wiggins, Russell Belk, Ruth Rentschler, and Danilo C. Dantas

For more information about this series, please visit: www.routledge.com/Discovering-the-Creative-Industries/book-series/DCI

Doing (and Using) Research in Arts and Cultural Management

François Colbert, Jennifer Wiggins, Russell Belk, Ruth Rentschler, and Danilo C. Dantas

Routledge
Taylor & Francis Group
LONDON AND NEW YORK

Designed cover image: Cathy Bélanger, Échos des Sommets II
(in English: Echoes from the summits II)

First published 2026
by Routledge
4 Park Square, Milton Park, Abingdon, Oxon OX14 4RN

and by Routledge
605 Third Avenue, New York, NY 10158

Routledge is an imprint of the Taylor & Francis Group, an informa business

British Library Cataloguing-in-Publication Data
A catalogue record for this book is available from the British Library

ISBN: 978-1-032-78452-6 (hbk)
ISBN: 978-1-032-78449-6 (pbk)
ISBN: 978-1-003-48795-1 (ebk)

DOI: 10.4324/9781003487951

Typeset in Caslon
by Apex CoVantage, LLC

Contents

PREFACE

This book offers a rich, critical, and engaging exploration of research methods for studying arts and cultural management. It is an informative resource for academics, including advanced masters' and PhD candidates, in areas such as arts and cultural management, creative industries, cultural policy, festivals and events, heritage, museum studies, arts consumption and marketing, and cultural tourism. It will also appeal to consultants, evaluators, and fundraisers who do research on a regular basis, as well as professional arts managers seeking to understand the changing landscape.

Moving beyond generic discussions of research methods, this book is structured around a framework that provides a process for undertaking arts and cultural management research. Readers are guided through the process of developing an interesting and relevant research question, conducting a thorough literature review selecting an appropriate methodology to answer the question, ensuring that the data collection and analysis are conducted rigorously and ethically, and communicating the resulting findings to an academic or managerial audience.

Perhaps uniquely, this book provides a strong foundation in both qualitative and quantitative research methods, as well as mixed methods approaches. The chapters include detailed guidelines for conducting surveys, interviews, experiments, case studies, and ethnographies, as well as literature reviews and data analysis. The emphasis is on selecting the right research method to answer the specified research question and approaching the research design, data collection, data analysis, and data presentation in a manner that will meet the requirements and expectations of that particular methodology.

The authors' goal is to offer a book simple enough to enlighten a beginner while covering the elements of constructing a rigorous research methodology. It is aimed at the neophyte, using simple, accessible language, but it is equally valuable for those with experience in research.

The chapters engage with both traditional and contemporary research topics, providing examples of high-quality research from national, regional, and local settings in various parts of the world.

The co-authors are five diverse scholars who are experienced not only in standard qualitative and quantitative methods, but also emerging techniques such as big data, netnography, and digital analysis. All five authors teach at post-graduate levels, having designed and delivered doctoral curricula at major international conferences and for higher education curricula. They are therefore familiar with the pitfalls and needs of research methods training for the readers of this book. Further, they have experience of working with practitioners in the arts and cultural management field. The book content can thus be adapted to the realities of the arts and cultural field, with examples used to guide the researcher in their research process.

They come together through this book, taking a deep dive into research methods, illustrating a process in clear, easy-to-read chapters with plenty of examples from their own and other scholars' experience. Book chapters were led by one author but reviewed and revised by others. François Colbert led Chapter 1 and Chapter 4, with Ruth Rentschler co-authoring them. Jennifer Wiggins led Chapters 2, 5, and 7, and co-authored Chapter 10. Russell Belk led Chapters 6, 9 and 10. Ruth Rentschler led Chapter 3 and co-authored Chapters 1, 4, and 8. Danilo C. Dantas led Chapter 8. All authors provided insights on each other's chapters to ensure the book presents as an integrated whole for the reader.

This book provides a thorough and comprehensive view of research methods, as well as ensuring a contemporary approach to doing (and using) arts and cultural management research. It is based on the co-authors' lifetime of experience working in academia and with industry, nonprofits, business, and government. This unique combination of co-authors makes the book an essential resource for arts and cultural management scholars, academics, research students, and reflective practitioners in the arts and cultural management field.

FIGURES, TABLES, TEXTBOXES, AND EXERCISES

Figures

Tables

Textboxes

Exercises

Acknowledgments

We acknowledge that this book project was undertaken by a group of scholars from different countries in the world. However, it takes more than five authors to write a book! While our dedication is written by the five co-authors, we wish to thank all those who made this book happen, from librarians to families and friends, colleagues and commentariat, as well as our pet dogs and cats.

Our supporting team

Throughout the writing process, the co-authors were supported by Terry Clague at Routledge and his extraordinary publishing assistants, Laura Slater and Naomi Round Cahalin. We thank them for their support of this book and the production team for taking to market.

1

FOUNDATIONS OF ARTS AND CULTURAL RESEARCH

What is research?

Any collection of data of any nature whatsoever for the purpose of better knowing the audience or understanding a managerial phenomenon can be called research. Research entails a set of activities in which researchers use various structured methods to contribute to the production of new knowledge, where knowledge may be theoretical, fundamental, or applied (Drolet et al., 2023, p. 270). Managers accumulate data on their market to adequately respond to consumer demand and obtain an edge on that market. Academics conduct fundamental research to try to explain phenomena related to audiences, individuals, and companies, as well as to management in general, and to suggest explanatory models of behavior. The academic researcher wants to enrich knowledge and contribute to its advancement, both for its own sake and for the communities they serve. These two types of research have distinct goals. Academics conduct fundamental research to try to explain phenomena related to governments, organizations, stakeholders as groups and/or individuals, as well as to society in general, and to suggest explanatory models of behavior.

The manager wants to solve a problem and find a short-term solution for the good of his company. The academic researcher wants to enrich knowledge and contribute to its advancement. Although the goal is different, the basic notion remains the same: it is about collecting data with

DOI: 10.4324/9781003487951-1

rigorous methods in order to avoid research bias and obtain relevant and valid data or knowledge. Of course, the type of approach may be different, more or less sophisticated, depending on the goal sought (Langley, 2009; Langley et al., 2013). This book is mainly intended for early career researchers starting their research journey and inquisitive practitioners in government, industry, or non-profits who have the responsibility of evaluating their programs and projects. It can also be used by managers who want to understand research methods that provide a rigorous data collection and information approach.

We position the chapter within the research methods field, stating our worldview that has governed the manner in which we discuss research methods in this book. The book is mainly intended for emerging researchers, such as those who are studying for a master's degree and starting a doctorate. It can also be used by managers who want to understand a scientific approach underlying rigorous and information search and data collection.

Academic research

The goal of academic research is to add to a body of knowledge on a given subject. Research evolves in small steps. The researcher focuses on a specific and circumscribed phenomenon. The results provide a perspective on the phenomenon studied that reflects the worldview of the researcher, moving from what we do know to examining what we do not know. Research methods can be undertaken from various perspectives. Each world view has its own challenges, ethically, theoretically, and practically (McGaw & Vance, 2023). The first thing that a research supervisor often does is to guide the student to limit the scope of their research study and to focus it on a worldview that is consistent with the research question they seek to answer. There is often a tendency for an emerging scholar to want to embrace too much.

The result of the academic work will be accessible to the research community in the form of a master's or doctoral thesis or an academic article. The structure of an article in the field of management follows a standard form. It will have roughly eight sections defined around a series of important terms of any research topic.

First, there will be an introduction that will serve to whet the reader's appetite. Writing an article should be seen as a narrative, a story that the researcher tells. Like any story, this one should be interesting. But unlike a story, the outcome should be given in the introduction to the work and briefly indicate how the research contributes new information to knowledge. That is why the introduction is usually written after the research has been completed. Here is what Summers (2001) says that an effective introduction should contain:

1) Position your paper in the field of your research, showing the importance of your subject, either for scientific knowledge and/or in terms of the industry's economic and social importance, or both.
2) State in general terms what has been done in the field under study.
3) Identify important gaps, inconsistencies, and/or controversies in the relevant literature.
4) Provide a concise statement of the manuscript's purpose, and the contribution the manuscript makes to the literature.

Then, the literature review serves to set the scene (see Chapter 4). Here, the researcher shows that they know the literature on their research topic in such a way as to clearly identify a gap in knowledge and the contribution that the study makes. The aim here is not to report on everything that has been published but to identify the boundaries that allow the research topic to be circumscribed.

A chapter will sometimes have a section that will propose one or more research questions or formulate research hypotheses based on the identified gap. Either in this section or in the previous one, it will proceed to the definition of the constructs or concepts used. Because it often happens that different authors have proposed a definition that is a little different for the same construct, it may be necessary to choose the one that is most appropriate for your research purpose and state why you use this one rather than another one.

Once the research questions or the hypotheses are well-defined, you then decide on the method to collect the data and justify its choice. If you are dealing with qualitative research, you explain the approach, you note how you analyzed it manually or whether you used software to make sense of the mass of accumulated text, and so forth (see Chapter 10). If you opt for quantitative analysis, you may choose a statistical model to analyze the results (see Chapters 2 and 5 to 9).

Sometimes you will find a section called "findings' or "results" in a chapter. This is usually a summary of the answers to the research question and their answers obtained through the study.

In the discussion section, we summarize what we found; we summarize how we filled the identified gap and state the contribution of the study to the body of knowledge.

All research has limits because each study examines only a portion of a phenomenon. There are always grey areas. The researcher highlights them to show that they are aware of them. Sometimes they explain again the worldview they adopted that caused them take a particular perspective of the phenomenon in order to be able to highlight one aspect over another one. Results can also raise other questions that should be explored in future research. The researcher shows the way for possible future research. This is important because it guides other researchers on how to take a study forward.

Information search from the manager's point of view

What a government department, nonprofit organization, or business usually looks for is information about its reputation, brand, or customers. Data is obtained from the institution or company's management information system (MIS) which, after analysis, provides data that can be turned into information for decision-making. Hence, it provides a fundamental element in the management process.

The MIS includes three types of data: internal data, secondary external data, and primary external data. Internal data is data found within the company itself: sales reports, information from financial reports, customer reports, data mining, etc. Secondary external data, published by public or private organizations, are available in the form of reports in libraries, on the Internet, or from organizations that publish them. Finally, primary external data comes from information that the company collects directly from the consumer. This collection, called "market research," "survey," "investigation," "evaluation," or "research consulting," can be carried out by the institution itself or by a specialized firm mandated for this purpose.

"Internal data" is any data or information that can be found within the institution that could be used for management decision-making. These data come from six key sources: 1) the governance, finance, and accounting systems, 2) sales reports, 3) traffic on the company's website (data mining), 4) the customer list, 5) institution personnel, and 6) surveys and studies already conducted by the institution. It should be noted that a survey, at the time it is conducted, is considered a collection of primary external data, but the report kept on file then becomes part of the internal data.

Secondary external data includes data published by government agencies, such as Statistics Canada or Statistics Denmark. It can also entail data by private companies, such as the German firm Statistica. They are useful for research managers, providing them with the information needed to describe the strategy and structure of an industry (Luckman et al., 2019); evaluate policy (Redaelli, 2020); understand the size and composition of a market (Colbert, 2020); determine whether governance processes and mechanisms meet strategic and legislative requirements (Rentschler, Reid & Donelli, 2025); and measure the size and evolution of demand for a product or service, such as an experience or cultural tourism offer (Richards, 2018). The main advantage of this type of data is that it is inexpensive to develop or to purchase and not time-consuming to use. Using secondary external data allows research managers to gather information in a relatively short time, whereas they would have to spend several weeks or months collecting and collating this information themselves through a market study, not to mention the significant sums they would have to spend. Secondary external data also helps guide the collection of primary data, as it helps to focus the development of research questions and hypotheses.

It is by directly questioning the target consumer that the company obtains primary external data; this collection of information is called "market research," a "survey," or a "poll." The manager can collect the data himself or entrust the research to a specialized firm. The task therefore consists of collecting relevant data with regard to a defined problem, analyzing the data, and then interpreting it in a way that is useful for decision-making.

The decision to collect primary external data is based on the value of the information to be obtained in relation to its cost. In other words, the research manager judges whether the operation to be undertaken justifies the effort and resources required. For example, in a for-profit company, spending $5,000 on a survey is useless if the information obtained saves the company less than $5,000, or if the financial risk associated with a decision is less than this amount. However, in a non-profit organization or government agency, where doing social good and contributing to community wellbeing are the goals, monetary decisions may not be the sole reason for decision-making in relation to research decisions.

Qualitative research

Qualitative research is typically used for exploratory research or in a field where little research has been undertaken on a particular phenomenon. Qualitative research essentially provides rich data for deep analysis (Miles & Huberman, 1994). It is not based on hypotheses or preconceived ideas. The findings obtained are generalized to theory but cannot be generalized to a population since participants may be too few. It is generally a flexible, unstructured, and qualitative method. Academic use of these approaches is much broader (as discussed in Chapter 3).

This type of research approach is used for various purposes: to better define a problem; to develop propositions to be tested in a later study; to generate ideas for new services or products; to gather initial reactions to a new concept; to evaluate a program or project; or to determine the criteria that come into play in choosing an installation, film, or show (see, for example: Azmat et al., 2018; Benghozi, Salvaldor & Simon, 2017; Schiuma, 2009). Mapping arts-based initiatives: Assessing the organizational value of the arts. London: Arts and Business.).

It also allows us to learn about the interests and vocabulary of the consumer. It offers the researcher and the manager the opportunity to familiarize themselves with an environment that is unfamiliar to them. As an example, let's say a heritage museum wants to verify the quality of their exhibitions of the commercial staging of history in order to boost cultural tourism, as it helps visitors better understand the past. The museum could use the technique of investigators as "mystery visitors" who visit the museum incognito in order to provide feedback on customer service. Findings are analyzed and used to improve aspects related to the quality of exhibitions to museum visitors, thus boosting the museum experience for them (for e.g., see Goulding, Saren & Pressey, 2018).

Several techniques can be used to conduct exploratory research: focus groups, in-depth individual interviews, case studies, observation, projection techniques, etc. In order to do this, one gets a sample that is not chosen randomly but rather based on its relevance and accessibility (see Chapter 6 for a lengthy discussion of the subject). The results from this collection of information can give guidance for further research or improvements in the management conduct.

Quantitative research

Quantitative research, sometimes called descriptive research, aims to obtain precise information on a given topic. It generally starts from a hypothesis that it seeks to confirm or refute. It is used when the problem to be examined is clear, the information needs are sufficiently precise, and the problem and variables have been clearly identified. Exploratory research often precedes it, because it helps to formulate the initial hypothesis and to better understand the parameters of the study.

While exploratory research usually provides qualitative and indicative results from a small number of respondents, descriptive research allows for quantitative analyses to be carried out on samples representative of the population. Being representative means having an appropriate sample size and collecting data using a random sample (where each member of the population under study has the same chance to be selected in the study).

For example, descriptive research can be used to determine the factors that come into play in the decision to purchase a theatre ticket for a given population. It can also help to draw up the socio-demographic profile of museum visitors or to know the characteristics of popular music listeners in a particular region.

The importance of writing clearly

It is essential that your manuscript is well-written. To achieve this, your thoughts must be precise, because a manuscript must not only be well-written but also concise and follow a rigorous logic. It is always a good idea, once you've written your first draft, to let it sit for a week or two, then re-read it with a critical eye, asking yourself whether the reader will understand what you're trying to say. Writing is a difficult exercise. You have to do it over and over again before you craft words into a story that holds together and reads well, and where the reader can follow the argument. A refereed journal article has to tell a story, but unlike a story, the reader has to know the ending right from the start. That's why you need to say at the start of your story what you've found out.

When you're satisfied with your manuscript, have one or two colleagues read it, and ask them to act as if they were reviewers for a refereed journal. Ask them to be demanding. This is a great way to anticipate reviewers' comments. It allows you to improve your text while increasing the chances of it being accepted for publication. By the way, when you submit your manuscript, don't be offended if it doesn't make the first round. It's rare that a manuscript isn't returned to the author to respond to both major and minor comments. When you read these comments, you may be frustrated. This is normal.

Let them mature for a day or two, then reread the comments, separating those that are easy to fix from those that are more substantial. Think of the exercise as a way of improving your manuscript. When you return the new version of the manuscript, it should be accompanied by a note in which you first thank the reviewers for their comments and then say how you have responded to each of their comments; you do this by taking each comment one by one and explaining how you have responded to it. This will make it easier for the reviewers when they come to read your new version. Remember that a good reviewer may take a day or two to read your manuscript and write comments. So don't get upset if you think they just don't get it. That may be the case. Then ask yourself how you could write the thing more clearly. If they didn't understand, perhaps when your article is published, your reader won't either. If you ever decide not to modify your text following a comment, tell the reviewer why. If you feel that what the reviewer is asking for is impossible, talk to the editor in charge of your section. He or she will recommend what to do.

How to use this book

This book is intended for the novice researcher who wants a basic guide to the main elements that make up research. Each chapter covers a particular topic and can be used as a standalone.

Chapter 2 explores the matter of research questions and research designs. It will discuss the various types of research questions – ex. process-oriented "how" questions vs. variance-oriented "why" questions, descriptive vs. predictive vs. causal questions, brief mention of mediators and moderators. The chapter will end with guidelines for linking research questions to research designs – something like an "If your question looks like X, go to chapter Y" approach.

All research must follow a code of ethics. Chapter 3 discusses this aspect. The chapter starts with three scenarios in research governance and ethical conduct which may occur in the arts and cultural management setting. They illustrate that there are philosophical debates about research governance and ethical conduct within, across, and between disciplines, as well as within communities, cultures, and cases. This chapter covers the growing need to provide research governance and ethical conduct for projects, why, what, and how it is done and also how to manage data in an age where transparency is ever-growing and journals and indeed individuals can ask for data to be provided to demonstrate compliance with ethical standards. It relates to undertaking research for the common good for the community rather than for oneself, building trust among participants and others, as well as creating a bond with readers of your research. The chapter then discusses research governance and data management, often overlooked in research projects in the social sciences. The chapter ends with a table of research governance and ethical issues with questions for researchers to ask themselves before they start a research project.

With Chapter 4, the reader will learn about literature search and literature review around the questions "What, Why, and How Writing a Literature Review." The chapter is divided into two parts; the first one is about your literature review for your thesis, dissertation, or scientific article. It explains the main elements that must be present in this section. First, how to cite the authors you found and want to include, then defining the boundaries of your research, the construct you use, how to find the gap, and the contribution highlighted by your enquiry. Second, the chapter discusses the different ways on how to build your bibliography. The second part explains briefly how a literature review can be a piece of research in itself and can be published as an article in a scientific journal.

Chapter 5 is about the topic of Survey Research. It presents guidelines for conducting good survey research, including questionnaire design, measure validation, sampling, and correlational and regression analysis. Some discussion of statistical control is also included. The chapter ends with a checklist for conducting a survey.

Chapter 6 presents guidelines for conducting good interviews, including sampling methods and approaches for finding participants, structured vs. semi-structured vs. unstructured approaches, developing interview guides, probing, some mention of interviewer effects, coding interview data manually and through software, and identification of themes.

Chapter 7 brings the reader through the guidelines for conducting good experiments, including stimuli development, experimental control, random assignment, lab vs. field vs. quasi-experimental designs, and comparison of group means through ANOVA or t-tests.

"Case Study" is the title of Chapter 8. The chapter discusses various forms of case studies and presents guidelines for conducting case study research, including the selection of appropriate cases, various data collection methods (observation, interviews, analysis of archival information), and qualitative analysis and grounded theory.

With Chapter 9, the author explains what doing an Ethnography means and what 'Participant Observation' is all about.

Finally, Chapter 10 concludes the book by talking about how to turn your research of any type into a presentation and or manuscript that can be submitted for publication.

References

Azmat, F., Ferdous, A., Rentschler, R., & Winston, E. (2018), "Arts-based initiatives in museums: Creating value for sustainable development," *Journal of Business Research*, 85, 386–395.

Benghozi, P. J., Salvador, E., & Simon, J. P. (2017), "The race for innovation in the media and content industries: Legacy players and newcomers: Lessons for policy makers from the video game and cinema industries," *The Journal of Arts Management, Law, and Society*, 47(5), 346–360.

Colbert, F. (2020), "Marketing the arts," in *Handbook of cultural economics* (3rd ed., pp. 320–328). Edward Elgar Publishing.

Drolet, M., Rose-Derouin, E., Leblanc, J., Ruest, M., & Williams-Jones, B. (2023), "Ethical issues in research: Perceptions of researchers, research ethics board members and research ethics experts," *Journal of Academic Ethics*, 21, 269–292.

Goulding, C., Saren, M., & Pressey, A. (2018), "'Presence' and 'absence' in themed heritage," *Annals of Tourism Research*, 71, 25–38.

Langley, A. (2009), "Studying processes in and around organizations," in *The Sage handbook of organizational research methods* (pp. 409–429). London: Sage.

Langley, A., Smallman, C., Tsoukas, H., & Van de Ven, A. H. (2013), "Process studies of change in organization and management: Unveiling temporality, activity, and flow," *Academy of Management Journal*, 56(1), 1–13.

Luckman, S., Sinha, R., Anderson, H., Rentschler, R., & Chalken, C. (2019), "'The devil is in the level': Understanding inequality in Australia's film, TV and radio industries," *Media International*, 1–16. https://doi.org/10.1177/1329878X19892772.

McGaw, J., & Vance, A. (2023), "Dissonance, disagreement, difference: Challenging thematic consensus to decolonise grounded theory," *International Journal of Qualitative Methods*, 22, 1–12.

Miles, M. B., & Huberman, A. M. (1994), *Qualitative data analysis: An expanded sourcebook*. Thousand Oaks: Sage.

Redaelli, E. (2020), "Understanding American cultural policy: The multi-level governance of the arts and humanities," *Policy Studies*, 41(1), 80–97.

Rentschler, R., Reid, W., & Donelli, C. (Eds.). (2025), *The Routledge companion of governance in the global arts world*. Routledge.

Richards, G. (2018), "Cultural tourism: A review of recent research and trends," *Journal of Hospitality and Tourism Management*, 36, 12–21.

Schiuma, G. (2009), *Mapping arts-based initiatives: Assessing the organizational value of the arts*. London: Arts and Business.

Summers, J.O. (2001), "Guidelines for conducting research and publishing in marketing: From conceptualization through the review process," *Academy of Marketing Science Journal*, 29(4), 405–415.

2

RESEARCH QUESTIONS AND RESEARCH DESIGNS

Introduction

Research begins with an idea, often inspired by a concept you read about in the literature, a behavior you observe among artists or audiences, a shift in the arts management environment, a strategy or tactic being adopted by an arts organization, or your own arts consumption or creation experience. Jaccard and Jacoby (2020) view the generation of research ideas as an inherently creative process that is in many ways akin to the development of new artistic ideas. The initial spark can come from any number of sources or experiences – the authors list 27 heuristics for generating creative research ideas – and may result in multiple ideas that must be critically evaluated to refine and focus them toward one "good idea." As with the creation of art, part of the critical evaluation of research ideas is to consider their potential audience. Jaccard and Jacoby (2020) recommend asking these questions as part of focusing your research idea:

1. Is this a new solution to an existing problem or is it a new problem?
2. What population does it apply to?
3. Why is it important?
4. What makes it interesting?

Being interesting is perhaps the most important criterion in the evaluation of a research idea. Bartunek, Rynes and Ireland's (2006) survey of *Academy*

DOI: 10.4324/9781003487951-2

of Management Journal editorial board members finds that research ideas are most likely to be perceived as interesting when they are counterintuitive, novel, rigorously studied, well written, have practical implications, and have the potential to be impactful. Barley (2006) suggests that the perception is more nuanced, arguing that "Academic papers are a bit like rock and roll bands: whether an audience finds them interesting is a matter of perspective, if not taste" (p. 16). Similar to one's taste in music, Barley suggests that individual audience members will not agree on which ideas are the most interesting, that perceiving an idea to be interesting is not the same as liking it and wanting to hear more, that being interesting does not always imply being important (he cites the musician Tiny Tim as an example), and that being interesting is difficult to describe and often comes down to a feeling or sensibility. Fundamentally, like a piece of artwork, a research idea should strive to capture the attention of a particular audience and lead them to think about the topic in a new or different way.

Once you have selected a research idea, it must be refined into a specific research question that has the potential to contribute to our understanding of the topic. While it can be tempting to jump straight from the research idea to the study, this often leads to research that is poorly focused, insufficiently specified, and unlikely to make a strong theoretical contribution. It is worthwhile to take the time to identify your potential contribution, clarify your research goal, formulate a good research question, and select the right design to answer your question. This chapter will describe the steps involved in this process.

Step 1: Identify your potential contribution

When evaluating a new research idea, before specifying a research question and research design, it is important to consider the potential contribution that this idea could make to our broader understanding of the topic. Research studies can make different types of contributions, and some studies can make more than one type of contribution. Understanding your potential contribution will help to determine the appropriate research question and methodology, as well as the appropriate audience and outlet for the communication of your research. Considering this question at this stage of the process will also help you to make more efficient and effective decisions about how you approach your research so that the potential benefit of conducting the study outweighs its costs in terms of time, money, effort, and other resources.

The majority of academic research strives to make a *theoretical contribution*, where the inferences drawn from the research findings change the way that we think about and understand the underlying theoretical constructs or the relationships between them. Researchers sometimes assume that a theoretical contribution requires them to create an entirely new theory, but this is actually quite rare in the literature. Rather, most research contributes to our understanding of existing theories by examining questions that help to expand, refine, or find the boundaries of the theory (Jaccard & Jacoby, 2020). For example, in Wiggins (2004), I adapted an existing theory from the literature on consumer information processing – the motivation, ability, and opportunity model – and applied it to audience development. In doing so, I showed that this theory better explained audience behavior and likelihood to attend than the previously proposed RAND model of audience development.

Whetten (1989) suggests that this is best approached by focusing not on the components of the theory ("what") or the context in which it is applied ("who," "where," or "when"), but rather on the underlying theoretical mechanism ("why") or the process through which it occurs ("how"). For example, researchers might introduce a new *moderator variable* that changes the predictions of the theory, finding circumstances in which the predicted effect might grow stronger or weaker, reverse direction, or even cease to occur, in which case the researcher has identified a boundary condition. For example, in Alexiou, Wiggins and Preece (2020), we proposed that the effects of a successful or failed crowdfunding campaign on an arts organization's ability to raise funds in the subsequent year would change depending on the organization's age. For young organizations, a successful crowdfunding campaign signals legitimacy and has a positive effect on future donations, while a failed campaign calls the organization's legitimacy into question and therefore has a negative effect. However, for established organizations, a successful crowdfunding campaign substitutes for other donations, therefore having a negative effect on future donations, while a failed campaign garners sympathy and actually increases future donations. Researchers might also propose a new understanding of the process through which a theoretical effect occurs, testing new *mediating variables* or providing a more in-depth understanding of the process over time. For example, in Cui and Wiggins (2017), we theorized that the reason that different ways of framing a pay-what-you-want message led to different chosen prices was because the message frames activated different mindsets in the consumer, and mindsets that were more altruistic or equity-minded, as opposed to egoistic, led to greater prices paid.

In some cases, the research question may be considering a phenomenon that cannot be explained by current theory, and a grounded or emergent theory approach is taken, in which the researcher seeks to understand the phenomenon from the perspective of the participants in order to allow new theoretical ideas to emerge from the resulting thick description. For example, in Baiocchi et al. (2024), my coauthors Danilo C. Dantas and François Colbert and their colleagues used an emergent approach to develop a theoretical understanding of how live music infrastructure and traditions help to shape a city's cultural identity from interviews and observations in two different global cities. Similarly, in Chandra and Belk (2024), my coauthor Russell Belk and his colleague develop a theoretical understanding as to how consumers value nonfungible tokens from in-depth interviews. Essentially, any research in which the inferences drawn from the study's findings provide new insights that change our current understanding of a theory has the potential to make a theoretical contribution.

Researchers sometimes seek to make a *methodological contribution*, where the focus is not on developing a new theoretical idea but rather on improving our ability to conduct research on an existing theoretical idea. For example, researchers might develop and validate a self-report scale that provides an improved measure of participants' perceptions or characteristics. For example, Bourgeon-Renault, Lagier and Bréhonnet (2024) develop a new scale to measure perceived artist authenticity, and Hernando and Campo (2017) develop one to measure an artist's perceived value as a brand. Researchers might also propose a stronger, more refined, or more parsimonious model to predict an outcome. For example, Ansari, Siddarth and Weinberg (1996) propose an extension to Venkatesh and Mahajan's (1993) model of bundle pricing to make it more appropriate for use in nonprofit industries, demonstrating that their new model fits better with data from a series of classical Indian music concerts. In both of these cases, the underlying theory does not change, but future researchers' ability to collect empirical data related to the theory is improved by these new methodological tools.

Finally, researchers may seek to make a *managerial contribution*. This is different from the managerial implications discussed at the end of an academic journal article that is primarily making a theoretical contribution, which is presented to demonstrate the relevance and realism of the theoretical idea. Research whose main goal is to make a managerial contribution might seek to identify best practices for arts organizations under a particular set of circumstances, or determine the effectiveness of a new strategy or tactic for the organization's success. If the inferences drawn from the study's findings are in the form of "therefore, the organization should engage in these behaviors in order to be more successful," then the contribution is primarily managerial. This is common and appropriate for many master's theses, consulting projects, and other forms of practice-oriented research, as well as for teaching case studies in which the goal is for future practitioners to learn from this specific situation and apply it to their own managerial decision making. However, this type of contribution is typically not sufficient for publication in an academic journal. If you are seeking an academic publication from your research, your goal should be to make a theoretical contribution.

In order to evaluate whether your research question has the potential to make a theoretical contribution, it is helpful to again think in terms of your future audience. Many researchers make broad references to contributing to "the literature" without thinking critically about who is most likely to read your research and be interested in your findings and conclusions. This is where the concept of a literature stream comes into play. A mentor of mine phrased it this way:

> Imagine your field as a giant cocktail party. All over the room are small groups of researchers talking to each other. Each group is having its own conversation about a specific idea that everyone in the group finds interesting. Your task is to choose which group you are going to join and think about what you are going to add to their conversation.

While there are moments at academic conferences that resemble this cocktail party, the mentor intended this as an analogy for the different streams of research that exist within a particular field's literature. A specific group of researchers will be studying the same topic, and any time one of them publishes a new article, they are communicating to the rest of the group and contributing to the ongoing conversation about the topic. When you choose to study a topic, you are necessarily joining one of these conversations, and it is important to consider what you will be adding as a contributor.

This requires you to have an in-depth understanding of the current conversation: what has already been discussed, and what is missing or yet to be found. This is why it is so important to conduct a thorough literature review on your topic before you start to design and implement your research studies. It is not necessary to read every article on a topic, particularly for highly researched topics, but it is essential to read enough to define the core constructs related to the topic, develop a mental model of their theoretical relationships to each other, get a sense of the development of the topic over time, and most importantly, understand the current state of the topic, the most recent findings, and their implications for the underlying theory. Chapter 4 discusses how to conduct a thorough literature search and literature review.

Once you understand the current conversation around the topic, ask yourself how you can move the conversation forward. Researchers are often instructed to seek a "gap" in the literature, which can lead to contribution statements that say, "No one has examined this idea yet so this study will." This is not enough to move the conversation forward. There must be a good reason to examine this new idea, and it must have implications that will change our understanding of the theory. Research that adds a new variable to an existing theory, for example, is often referred to as making an incremental contribution, which may not be sufficient to engage your audience's attention and persuade them that your research is interesting. On the other hand, it is usually not wise to attack a theory wholesale or argue against its underlying principles, particularly when it is well established in the literature. In Davis's highly cited (1971) article on what makes research interesting, he suggests that the best approach is not to challenge research findings outright, but rather to challenge the assumptions behind those findings. For example, in Alexiou and Wiggins (2022), we noted extensive findings in the literature that while artists acknowledge the value of business skills, they are resistant to acquiring such skills. We argued that this is due to the association of business skills with a market orientation, whose commercial logic conflicts with the artist identity, and that an entrepreneurial orientation that emphasizes autonomy, innovativeness, and proactiveness would have less conflict with an artistic logic. Our findings that framing the relevant skills as entrepreneurial increases artists' willingness to participate in educational programs did not directly challenge prior negative findings, but rather enhanced our understanding of why these findings occurred and how they might be overcome.

I like to ask myself four questions to critically evaluate my potential contribution before I undertake a new research project. I usually ask these questions about academic researchers having a theoretical conversation, but they can also be applied to a managerial or educational audience with the same effect.

1. Who am I talking to?
2. What are they talking about?
3. What am I adding to the conversation?
4. Why should they care about what I am saying?

The fourth question is contingent on the first three, but it is the most important to answer. If you cannot find a reason why the researchers currently studying this topic would be interested in what you are adding to the conversation, then you do not have a strong enough contribution.

Step 2: Clarify your research goal

Once you have identified a potential theoretical contribution, it is important to clarify the goal of your research project. There are five goals that can be accomplished through empirical research: the research can seek to describe, explain, predict, test causes of, or understand a phenomenon. Each of these goals has the potential to make a theoretical contribution to the literature on the phenomenon, but clarifying your specific goal is helpful in making the transition from idea to research question.

In a sense, all research begins with description. We describe the context in which the research takes place, the sample of participants, the procedures and limitations of the design, and the phenomenon itself. We also begin our data analysis with descriptive statistics or other ways of describing what we have found before we begin to interpret it. This type of description is usually the first step in the process toward one of the other four goals.

Research that has description as its primary goal, on the other hand, seeks to develop a thick description that gives the reader as complete a picture of the phenomenon as possible, in the time, place, and context in which it occurs. You might think, for example, of historical research that describes the past with a richness that enables the reader to imagine what it would have been like to experience these events themselves. For example, in Rentschler, Lee and Subramaniam, (2021), my coauthor Ruth Rentschler and her colleagues conduct a historical analysis of the practices of a national arts council that funds arts organizations and artists to understand how the council uses its budgets, funding distributions, and organizational disclosures to both establish its legitimacy and respond to changing perceptions of the legitimacy of art and entertainment over time. Or you might think of a narrative inquiry that seeks to tell the story of particular people from their own point of view and in doing so sheds light on a phenomenon through the eyes of its participants. In Azmat et al. (2023), Ruth and her colleagues draw on interviews, site visits, and observations to describe how small non-profit arts organizations cope with the tensions surrounding their social responsibility efforts. Or perhaps you might think of a case study that documents and analyzes an organization's response to a particular set of circumstances or how they responded to a strategic dilemma. In Rentschler, Lee and Subramaniam (2023), Ruth and her colleagues conduct a case study of the Adelaide Festival to understand how the organization has adapted its governance mechanisms to a series of crises. Descriptive research is sometimes framed in research methods textbooks as a preliminary step, which should be followed by studies with a different goal, but it is a research goal in and of itself if the resulting description is rich enough that the reader will learn something new from experiencing the story.

Research with a goal to explain is often looking for the boundaries of when, where, or under what circumstances the phenomenon of interest occurs. You might imagine a regression model in which the goal is to test whether each of the independent variables leads to significant variation in the dependent variable, or perhaps a structural model that focuses on mediator variables that explain the process through which the independent variable is related to specific outcomes. For example, researchers may be trying to understand when an organization is more likely to make one strategic decision over another, or under what circumstances a strategy will or will not have a positive effect on the organization's performance. In Johnson and Ellis (2011), we looked at arts presenters' message strategy for communicating with potential donors, as well as the benefits they offered at different donation levels, to see how they influenced audience members' willingness to donate and attributions of their own motivations to donate. Researchers might also consider the characteristics of individuals that make them more or less likely to attend arts performances or to support the arts financially. For example, in d'Astous et al. (2008), my coauthor François Colbert and his colleagues conducted a survey of consumers across five countries and found that their perceptions of different countries as producers of cultural products are explained by factors such as familiarity, openness to foreign cultures, home country bias, and proximity. Segmentation studies, such as Gürel and Nielsen's (2019) study of art museum visitors, are another example of explanatory research, seeking to understand what drives groups of audience members to exhibit different arts consumption behaviors. A comparative case study, such as Alshawaaf and Lee's (2024) study of corporate sponsorship across two countries, might also have an explanatory goal to explain the circumstances that led to outcome A for organization C and outcome B for organization D when they were facing the same environment or strategic decision.

Research with a goal to predict is also typically seen in a regression-based format, but the focus is on maximizing the predictive power of the model overall, as opposed to testing the explanatory value of any given independent variable. In simple terms, predictive research seeks to find the combination of independent variables that best predict observed outcomes on the dependent variable. For example, this approach is common in research focused on finding the variables that best predict the box office performance of films, as in Sawhney and Eliashberg (1996) or commercial theater productions, as in Reddy, Swaminathan and Motley (1998), and in research on dynamic pricing that seeks to develop models that are better able to predict audience demand and willingness to pay for tickets, as in Lévy-Garboua and Montmarquette (1996) or Urrutiaguer (2002).

Research that seeks to test causal relationships will always be experimental, as experiments are the only method that meets the requirements for demonstrating causality, as discussed in Chapter 7. This research can take on two forms. The first approach seeks to examine causes of an effect, manipulating different independent variables alone or interacting with each other to see which combination of variables leads to the effect of interest. For example, in Alexiou and Wiggins (2022), we used an experiment to examine which components of an entrepreneurial orientation made artists more willing to pursue educational opportunities that focused on entrepreneurial skills over those that focused on business schools. Essentially, this research strives to answer the question of why the phenomenon occurs. The second approach seeks to examine the effects of a cause, often measuring multiple dependent variables to see what outcomes vary based on changes in the independent variable. For example, in Wiggins et al. (2017), we experimentally tested the impact of different strategies arts organizations use to respond to negative reviews on consumers' attitude towards the response, attitude towards the arts organization, and likelihood of attending a performance. It is important to note that research testing causal relationships does not draw conclusions in the form of "we have proven that X is the definitive cause of Y," but rather, "when X occurs, or when the organization does X, then Y is more likely to occur, and we are confident that this is a result of X and not an artifact of other factors." This need to eliminate alternative explanations is why this type of research requires an experimental design.

Finally, research that seeks to understand a phenomenon focuses on questions relating to how a phenomenon arises and how it is perceived and experienced by its participants. Rather than focusing on the variables that can explain, predict, or cause the phenomenon, the goal is instead to grasp the experience of the phenomenon from the perspective of the individuals who are involved with it. This can only be achieved through engaging the participants directly in the research and asking open-ended questions that enable them to speak in their own words, which is why this type of research is usually approached through methods such as depth interviews or ethnography. Research focused on understanding enables researchers to uncover ideas or perspectives that would not have been predicted by existing theory. This can result in the emergence of new theoretical ideas, or it can highlight the exceptional cases and situations where existing theory does not apply. It can also provide a depth of understanding of participants' lived experiences that is not possible to achieve through research that seeks to develop a generalizable model that applies to a broad range of the population.

Any given research idea can be approached with multiple research goals and methods. For example, my coauthor Russell Belk and I both study the phenomenon of psychological ownership, the feeling that something belongs to you even if you cannot legally own it (Pierce, Kostova & Dirks, 2001). However, we approach it in different ways. In my recent work, I have used surveys and experiments to determine whether members of a brand or fan community's perceived ownership of the brand, for example, Swifties' perceived ownership of Taylor Swift and her music, increases their likelihood to engage in actions that help the brand or the community and changes how they interact with other community members (Kuchmaner, Wiggins & Grimm, 2019, 2024; Kuchmaner, Wiggins & Lyndall, 2025). In his recent work, Russ has used depth interviews to develop a deeper understanding of how consumers perceive ownership or psychological possession of intangible objects of value, including purchases made using cashless apps versus physical cash (Khan & Belk, 2024) and intangible art forms such as non-fungible tokens, or NFTs (Chandra & Belk, 2024). Our different research goals lead us to different research questions and methodological approaches, but we are both contributing to our field's overall knowledge of this phenomenon. Indeed, Pierce, Kostova and Dirks' (2001) study that sought to explain psychological ownership was grounded in the understanding provided by Russ's study of possessions as an extension of the self (Belk, 1988), and both articles are viewed as seminal works in this literature stream.

Step 3: Specify your research question

Now that you have articulated your research goal, the next step is to specify your research question. Your research question should be broad enough to encompass the full scope of your research goal but narrow enough to enable you to design a study that will answer it. Scholars have offered numerous guidelines for specifying a research question. Valuable discussions can be found, for example, in Van de Ven (2007), Kerlinger and Lee (2000), and Creswell and Creswell (2018). Integrating their recommendations, we can arrive at a set of parameters for specifying good research questions:

1. *Make sure that your research question is a question.* Researchers often make the mistake of specifying statements or hypotheses of what they expect to find rather than a true question. Another version of this is to frame the research question such that the only possible answers are "yes" and "no," for example, "Does X increase Y?" This approach is too limiting at this stage of the process and may lead the researcher to miss potential ideas or opportunities. Good research questions are broad, open-ended, and able to be answered in multiple ways.
2. *Start your research question with* how *or* why. Questions that begin with *who, where,* or *when* are focused on elements of the context, not the concepts, rendering them too narrow and specific for research ideas that have the potential to make a theoretical contribu-

tion. Questions that begin with *what* may be appropriate, but they are likely to be combined with questions that ask either *how* or *why* to fully accomplish their research goal.

3. *Focus your research question on a specific phenomenon or concept.* While it is important for research questions to be broad, they must still be focused on the phenomenon or concept of interest to avoid the question extending beyond the scope of what is possible in a study. This is also an opportunity to ensure that your research question is directly addressing the problem that you have identified or observed and will therefore make the contribution you intend. It may be valuable at this stage to consider several possible answers to your research question that your empirical findings may reveal and whether your idea would still be interesting.
4. *Craft several follow-up subquestions that reflect your research goal.* If your goal is to describe or understand a phenomenon, this is when questions that ask *what, who, where,* and *when* are appropriate to narrow the focus of the research in service of the overall research question. If your goal is to explain, predict, or test the causes of a phenomenon, this is when you should specify the constructs that will be the focus of the study and their relationships to each other in a way that can give rise to testable hypotheses. Research questions that have a goal to describe or understand are necessarily broader than those that have a goal to explain, predict, or test cause, and are not expected to include references to variables or hypothesized relationships. However, it is still essential to begin this type of research with clearly specified research questions, even if the nature of the questions themselves suggests a more open-ended, exploratory, or emergent approach to the research.
5. *Expect your research question to evolve and change over the course of your research.* Fundamentally, research is an iterative process. Your initial research question may change as your understanding of the topic or phenomenon grows, for example, as you review the literature, design the details of your empirical study, and uncover initial findings. This is not to suggest that you should engage in post hoc theorizing and pretend to have predicted a finding that you did not, but rather that your research question will evolve as you learn.

Combining these recommendations can lead to the creation of research questions resembling the examples in Textbox 2.1.

> ***Textbox 2.1 Examples of research questions***
>
> How do the messages communicated to donors and the benefits they receive for their donations influence donors' attributions about their own motivations for donating? (Johnson & Ellis, 2011)
>
> How does the framing of a pay-what-you-want message influence consumers' chosen prices? Can this difference be explained by the different message frames activating different mindsets? Which message framing – pay-what-you-want, pay-what-you-can, or pay-what-you-think-it's-worth – provides the most benefit to the firm? (Cui & Wiggins, 2017)
>
> Why are artists more willing to pursue educational opportunities to acquire entrepreneurial skills than business skills? Can this difference be explained by perceptions of the legitimacy of these educational programs? What aspects of entrepreneurial orientation contribute to this difference? (Alexiou & Wiggins, 2022)

It may also be valuable during this process is to consider whether your research is fundamentally a variance model or a process model, a dichotomy proposed by Van de Ven (2007). As he explains, variance models are focused on answering "what" or "why" questions that examine the antecedents or consequences of a particular phenomenon, while process models are focused on answering "how" questions that examine the emergence, development, growth, or termination of a phenomenon over time. In other words, variance models investigate questions of "what causes what" or "what influences what," while process models investigate questions of "how do things develop and change over time" (p. 146). These two different types of research questions lend themselves naturally to different research methodologies and research designs.

Step 4: Select your research design

Once you have identified your potential contribution, clarified your research goal, and specified your research question, it is finally time to select a research design. In some cases, the choice of research methodology is defined by the research goal, for example, research intended to test cause must use an experimental method. More typically, multiple research designs can be used to answer the same research question, and determining the appropriate design depends on how the researcher frames the research question, the research goal, and the intended contribution.

Research methods are often broadly classified into quantitative and qualitative methods, which have been differentiated in a variety of ways from the simplest "is the data in numbers or words" to complex discussions of the philosophy of science underlying each approach. Much of the latter conversation occurred at the end of the 20th century and is rather outdated in our current environment, in which it is generally accepted that knowledge is fragmented, meaning is socially constructed, and truth is relative to the perception of each individual. However, the difference is not as simple as the form of the data either. Quantitative and qualitative approaches to research differ in several fundamental ways that map onto the research goals outlined earlier. These differences are detailed in Table 2.1.

Quantitative research seeks to generalize the inferences derived from empirical findings beyond the specific context of the research study. This type of approach is seeking generalities, descriptions of typical behavior of the population or likely outcomes of particular events or strategies. This research takes an external perspective, with the researcher acting as an outside observer, and usually develops theoretical predictions prior to data collection that are then tested through the data analysis. It is important to note that it is not the findings themselves that are being generalized in quantitative

Table 2.1 Differences between quantitative and qualitative research

Quantitative Research	**Qualitative Research**
Seeks generalizability beyond the context of the research study	Seeks specificity to the context of the research study
Takes the perspective of the researcher as an outside observer	Takes the perspective of the participant as an inside observer
Theory exists prior to data collection and is tested through data analysis	Theory emerges from the data collection and data analysis process
More appropriate for a variance model	More appropriate for a process model
Research seeks to explain, predict, or test causes of a phenomenon	Research seeks to richly describe or understand a phenomenon

research, but rather the implied theoretical relationships that they represent. As such, quantitative research is more appropriate for variance models and best suited to research with a goal to explain, predict, or test causes.

Qualitative research seeks to elaborate on a phenomenon within its context of place and time. This type of approach is seeking specifics, as opposed to generalizations, and does not expect the findings to be valid beyond the specific context in which the phenomenon is studied. Rather, the goal is to take an internal perspective and present the phenomenon as it is experienced and understood by the participants, and to let theoretical implications of the findings emerge from the data rather than specifying them ahead of time. As such, qualitative research is more appropriate for process models and best suited to research with a goal to describe or understand.

Viewed in this manner, quantitative and qualitative research do not substitute for each other, nor do they inherently conflict with each other. Rather, they are complementary approaches to research that ask different research questions and pursue different research goals. A phenomenon of interest may be primarily studied through quantitative methods, qualitative methods, or both, depending on the nature of the phenomenon and the relevant research questions surrounding it.

It is also worth noting that some research questions may be best answered through mixed methods designs. Creswell and Creswell (2018) identify three different approaches to mixing quantitative and qualitative methods to answer a research question:

1. *Exploratory Sequential Mixed Methods Design:* the researcher begins with open-ended questions and qualitative inquiry, then uses the findings to develop theoretical hypotheses that are tested using quantitative methods such as surveys or experiments.
2. *Explanatory Sequential Mixed Methods Design:* the researcher begins by collecting quantitative data to establish the phenomenon, then follows with qualitative inquiry to better understand how the phenomenon occurs or is perceived by participants.
3. *Convergent Mixed Methods Design:* the research collects and analyzes quantitative and qualitative data around the phenomenon and compares the findings to determine if they converge on the same underlying theoretical idea or understanding.

Most researchers are trained in either quantitative or qualitative research and do not feel comfortable using the opposite methods, which is appropriate. Both approaches to research require extensive knowledge and training, and neither is simpler or easier than the other. However, it is important not to let the researcher's experience be the primary driver of the research design that is chosen. There is a tendency for methods to act as blinders, leading researchers to view their ideas and research questions through the lens of the method they are most comfortable with or accustomed to using. For example, I have seen researchers develop a theoretical model that proposes a set of antecedent and consequence relationships between variables, and then "test" their model with a case study. This is not an appropriate method for this research goal, and therefore not a valid empirical study. Instead, let the research goal and research question drive the choice of research method. If the best method to answer the research question and make a potential contribution is one that the researcher is less familiar with, the researcher can seek out training or coauthors who are experienced with the method, or they can change the research question to be consistent with the method in which they have experience. What is essential is that the research method match the research question.

With this in mind, it is important to consider the variety of design options that are available to answer your research question and accomplish your research goal. Table 2.2 details design options that can potentially answer each of the research goals discussed earlier.

Table 2.2 Research goals and potential research designs

If your goal is to:	You might collect your data through:	Which can be found in:
Describe a phenomenon	Depth Interviews	Chapter 6
	Case Studies	Chapter 8
	Ethnography	Chapter 9
Explain a phenomenon	Surveys	Chapter 5
	Experiments	Chapter 7
	Comparative Case Studies	Chapter 8
Predict a phenomenon	Surveys	Chapter 5
	Experiments	Chapter 7
Test causes of a phenomenon	Experiments	Chapter 7
Understand a phenomenon	Depth Interviews	Chapter 6
	Case Studies	Chapter 8
	Ethnography	Chapter 9

Which specific design is most appropriate for your research study depends on the research question you have specified, the phenomenon you are studying, and the context in which your study will take place. It is a good idea to consider multiple research designs in the planning phase to determine which design will be most appropriate to answer your research question.

Conclusion

A research study is only as good as its design, and a research design is only as good as its underlying research question. Taking the time at the beginning of the research process to clearly identify a potential contribution, clarify a research goal, specify a research question, and select an appropriate research design increases the study's theoretical and methodological rigor, which is key to the study's ability to be published and potential impact. It is important to note that this is often an iterative process, with decisions about the research goal and research question refining the potential contribution, decisions about the research design refining the research question and research goal, and so on. It is also important to reiterate that no one research design is better or worse than the others and there is no "correct" way to conduct empirical research. Rather, each research design option will be more or less appropriate to answer a specified research question, strive for a particular research goal, and be consistent with a particular stream of literature to which the researcher wishes to contribute.

References

Alexiou, K., & Wiggins, J. (2022), "Legitimating business skills in fine arts education: The role of entrepreneurial orientation," *International Journal of Arts Management*, 24(3), 4–20.

Alexiou, K., Wiggins, J., & Preece, S. B. (2020), "Crowdfunding acts as a funding substitute and a legitimating signal for nonprofit performing arts organizations," *Nonprofit and Voluntary Sector Quarterly*, 49(4), 827–848.

Alshawaaf, N., & Lee, S. H. (2024), "The paradox of corporate sponsorship of arts in the age of austerity," *International Journal of Arts Management*, 26(2), 4–24.

Ansari, A., Siddarth, S., & Weinberg, C. B. (1996), "Pricing a bundle of products or services: The case of nonprofits," *Journal of Marketing Research*, 33(February), 86–93.

Azmat, F., Rentschler, R., Lee, B., & Fujimoto, Y. (2023), "Understanding social responsibility and relational pressures in nonprofit organisations," *Human Relations*. https://doi.org/10.1177/00187267231183852.

Baiocchi, A., Dantas, D. C., Pessôa, L. A. G. de P., & Colbert, F. (2024), "Cultural branding of cities: The role of live music in building a city's brand," *Cultural Trends*, 1–19. https://doi.org/10.1080/09548963.2024.2345836.

Barley, S. R. (2006), "When I write my masterpiece: Thoughts on what makes a paper interesting," *Academy of Management Journal*, 49(1), 16–20.

Bartunek, J. M., Runes, S. L., & Ireland, R. D. (2006), "What makes management research interesting, and why does it matter?," *Academy of Management Journal*, 49(1), 9–15.
Belk, R. W. (1988), "Possessions and the extended self," *Journal of Consumer Research*, 15(September), 139–168.
Bourgeon-Renault, D., Lagier, J., & Bréhonnet, R. (2024), "A scale for measuring perceived artist authenticity: When artists are associated with brands," *International Journal of Arts Management*, 27(1), 52–68.
Chandra, Y., & Belk, R. (2024), "Is that JPEG worth 70 million dollars? Value creation and perceptions of nonfungible tokens in a bubble economy," *Journal of Marketing Management*, 40(17/18), 1602–1633.
Creswell, J. W., & Creswell, J. D. (2018), *Research design: Qualitative, quantitative, and mixed methods approaches*. Los Angeles: Sage.
Cui, A. P., & Wiggins, J. (2012), "What you ask changes what I pay: Framing effects in pay what you want pricing," *Journal of Marketing Theory and Practice*, 25(4), 323–339.
d'Astous, A., Giraud Voss, Z., Colbert, F., Carù, A., Caldwell, M., & Courvoisier, F. (2008), "Product-country images in the arts: A multi-country study," *International Marketing Review*, 25(4), 379–403. https://doi.org/10.1108/02651330810887459.
Davis, M. S. (1971), "That's interesting: Towards a phenomenology of sociology and a sociology of phenomenology," *Philosophy of the Social Sciences*, 1(4), 309–344.
Gürel, E., & Nielsen, A. (2019), "Art museum visitor segments: Evidence from Italy on omnivores and highbrow univores," *International Journal of Arts Management*, 21(2), 55–69.
Jaccard, J., & Jacoby, J. (2020), *Theory construction and model-building skills*. New York: The Guilford Press.
Johnson, J. W., & Ellis, B. (2011), "The influence of messages and benefits on donors' attributed motivations: Findings of a study with 14 American performing arts presenters," *International Journal of Arts Management*, 13(2), 4–15.
Kerlinger, F. N., & Lee, H. B. (2000), *Foundations of behavioral research*. Harcourt College Publishers.
Khan, J., & Belk, R. (2024), "Money you could touch: Cash and psychological ownership," *Qualitative Market Research: An International Journal*, 27(5), 820–840.
Kuchmaner, C. A., Wiggins, J., & Grimm, P. E. (2019), "The role of network embeddedness and psychological ownership in consumer responses to brand transgressions," *Journal of Interactive Marketing*, 47, 129–143.
Kuchmaner, C. A., Wiggins, J., & Grimm, P. E. (2024), "In it together: Brands benefit after a transgression when perceived as co-owners of the brand community," *Journal of Marketing Management*, 40(3–4), 190–216.
Kuchmaner, C. A., Wiggins, J., & Lyndall, M. (2025), "Infringement on one is infringement on all: Observers experience vicarious territorial infringement in virtual brand communities," *Psychology & Marketing*, 42, 2509-2523.
Lévy-Garboua, L., & Montmarquette, C. (1996), "A microeconometric study of theatre demand," *Journal of Cultural Economics*, 20, 25–50.
Pierce, J. L., Kostova, T., & Dirks, K. T. (2001), "Toward a theory of psychological ownership in organizations," *Academy of Management Review*, 26(2), 298–310.
Reddy, S. K., Swaminathan, V., & Motley, C. M. (1998), "Exploring the determinants of broadway show success," *Journal of Marketing Research*, 35, 370–383.
Rentschler, R., Lee, B., & Subramaniam, N. (2021), "Calculative practices and socio-political tensions: A historical analysis of entertainment, arts and accounting in a government agency," *Accounting History*.
Rentschler, R., Lee, B., & Subramaniam, N. (2023), "Festival innovation in times of crisis," *Event Management*, 27, 559–575, special issue on Event Innovation and Resilience During Uncertainty. https://doi.org/10.3727/152599522X16419948695062.
Sawhney, M. S., & Eliashberg, J. (1996), "A parsimonious model for forecasting gross box-office revenue of motion pictures," *Marketing Science*, 113–131.

Urrutiaguer, D. (2002), "Quality judgements and demand for French public theatre," *Journal of Cultural Economics*, 22, 185–202.
Van de Ven, A. H. (2007), *Engaged scholarship: A guide for organizational and social research.* Oxford University Press.
Venkatesh, R., & Mahajan, V. (1993), "A probabilistic approach to pricing a bundle of services," *Journal of Marketing Research*, 30(4), 509–521.
Whetten, D. A. (1989), "What constitutes a theoretical contribution?," *Academy of Management Review*, 14(4), 490–495.
Wiggins, J. (2004), "Motivation, ability, and opportunity to participate: A reconceptualization of the RAND model of audience development," *International Journal of Arts Management*, 7(Fall), 22–33.
Wiggins, J., Song, C., Trivedi, D., & Preece, S. B. (2017), "Consumer perceptions of arts organizations' strategies for responding to critique," *International Journal of Arts Management*, 20(1), 4–20.

3

Doing ethics in arts and cultural management research

Scenarios

- I am a young researcher. I need to collect information that is sensitive and might make participants feel embarrassed or concerned about sharing it with me. How can I ask for this information in a respectful manner? How can I gain participant trust?
- A researcher wants to study children who have developed an interest in arts and cultural products. How does she manage informed consent?
- I am collecting data online where my participant usernames or IP addresses are linked to what they say. How do I preserve their privacy and anonymity? How do I handle potential ethical complaints to the university ethics office?
- A researcher sought to submit his paper to a quality academic journal. He noticed the statement on the journal website:
  - We seek to ensure content we publish is ethically sound. Authors need to provide an ethical statement with institutional approval and the ethics committee approval number, ensuring it complies with relevant guidelines for studies involving humans. Any work submitted without a suitable ethical statement of informed consent for all participants will be returned to the authors.
  - What is he to do to avoid such an ethical dilemma?

DOI: 10.4324/9781003487951-3

Introduction

Doing ethics in arts and cultural management research is as important in your research study as it is in daily life (Alvesson & Stephens, 2024). The ethical dilemmas at the beginning of this chapter illustrate real cases, showing how important it is (Zigmund, 1994). The scenarios are taken from the daily life of researchers. They cover issues about respect, trust, and responsibility and accountability in research, which are covered in this chapter. You may know of scenarios similar to these ones. The scenarios have been modified to ensure anonymity. Research institutions, like universities, try to avoid ethical dilemmas through institutional guidelines for researchers. But they are not sufficient when a researcher is considering what to do. Researchers need to think beyond what is required to what the right thing to do is.

These dilemmas illustrate how there are blurred boundaries between research governance and ethical conduct, meaning decisions on them are not always black and white (Alvesson & Stephens, 2024; Martino & Schormans, 2018). The boundaries are constantly changing. This chapter seeks to provide support to researchers before undertaking a study, to avoid ethical dilemmas like these.

Ethical research requires individual researchers, the community they serve, and the research institutions in which they work to be ethically responsible and accountable before, during, and after undertaking a research project. But sometimes, those same scholars have received little professional development or guidance in the processes and techniques of research governance and ethical conduct. Often, particular disciplines in universities lag behind medicine and science in how they 'do' research ethics. Hence, scholars are left to fend for themselves in order to learn what to do, why, when, and how to do it.

Hence, the purpose of this chapter is to provide scholars with support and understanding of the issues in how to 'do' ethics that will prompt further investigation into roles and responsibilities in relation to it. Research ethics entails the systems, dynamics, and processes that surround the research process, ensuring it is trustworthy, authentic, and robust.

Ethical – or indeed unethical – conduct relates to how each member of the research team behaves in relation to the study undertaken. Ethical conduct is defined as setting the moral tone for a researcher (Drolet et al., 2023), ensuring they are to be aware of the continuum on which ethical issues can occur. Ethical issues can be major or minor or somewhere in between. Ethical conduct can be compromised due to internal and external pressures, power relations, and social acceleration (or trying to do more with less in a competitive academic environment). It can occur due to lack of knowledge of research ethics, or due to institutions not providing training, mentoring, or professional development for researchers but expecting them to have gathered that information isomorphically, at different points in their research journey. Furthermore, research ethics is changing rapidly, requiring researchers to remain vigilant in understanding contemporary norms.

The rest of this chapter is structured as follows: This short chapter cannot examine all matters in research governance and ethical conduct. It focuses on introducing major sources of ethical dilemmas. Then it provides an ethical framework to structure your research study. In discussing the framework, seven steps in the ethical research process are outlined. Then the key topics of building trust, gaining participant respect, and being responsible and accountable are examined. The chapter then ends with the conclusion.

Ethical dilemmas

As the scenarios at the beginning of this chapter demonstrate, there are a multiplicity of ethical dilemmas that researchers may face every day, conditioned by varying roles undertaken by researchers, institutions, participants, and the community (Drolet et al., 2023). Next, let's discuss the key types of ethical dilemmas that may results in ethical breaches.

Types of ethical dilemmas

An ethical dilemma is a problem where a researcher is confronted with two courses of action, each of which may entail transgressing an ethical principle. Hence, neither solution is straight-forward or clear. This can make decision-making in research projects difficult, stressful, and emotionally draining. Traditionally, three key ethical dilemmas are considered of most concern (Mumford et al., 2010): falsification of data, fabrication of data, and plagiarism. Each is now explained.

1. *Falsification* is altering or misrepresenting the data in the study by, for example, manipulating images, changing or selectively omitting data points, or manipulating equipment or research processes to alter the findings for a desired effect.

2. *Fabrication* is making up data. The data were not present in your data set, whether that be interviews, surveys, or online posts, for example. Data fabrication occurs when researchers did not conduct a study described, or collect data that were recorded in their study.
3. *Plagiarism* entails copying another researcher's work and using their words in your own publications, without due recognition of that researcher. Plagiarism has different meanings in different cultural and ethnic traditions. The Western notion of plagiarism may not be understood by researchers from different cultural backgrounds, where they honor past researchers by using their material. Sometimes, a novice researcher may be accused of plagiarism, not out of malfeasance, but because they did not know what it was. There are well-documented cultural differences in what is considered unethical behavior when it comes to plagiarism, with Western academia having standards that are a dramatic shift for researchers from other cultural backgrounds. It is important to understand plagiarism in the context in which you are conducting your study.

Sources of ethical dilemmas are many and varied. Researchers function in a complex and competitive environment, where they can work under time and resource constraints, which puts them under undue pressure. Ethical dilemmas can arise due to perceived fabrication, falsification, and plagiarism (Mumford et al., 2010), or even cultural differences in ethical background (Kopec, 2023; Rentschler et al, 2020; Winter & Lavis, 2020).

Types of ethical breaches

Ethical dilemmas can lead to ethical breaches. Ethical breaches entail making a decision to take the wrong path in relation to an ethical matter. It means that a researcher has deviated from the agreed ethical standards or principles in the arts and cultural research field. The reason a researcher may be accused of an ethical breach could be due to an additional three matters: conflict of interest, status asymmetries, and publish or perish. We now turn to each of these concepts and briefly outline their importance.

1. *Conflict of interest* is defined as a scenario where personal interests and professional interests collide, potentially or actually compromising researcher judgment, decisions, or actions in a study. It is considered a serious conflict if there may be personal gain, espe-

cially monetary gain, from the position in which the researcher finds themselves. It could be that an academic colleague unduly influenced another academic colleague to falsify, fabricate, or plagiarize material. Such a scenario may occur when two researchers have different objectives, with one of them influenced unduly by the other in a way that provides that person with an unfair advantage or quick access to a publication. It may not be possible to eliminate conflicts of interest. But it is possible to manage it or to declare it.

2. *Status asymmetries* is understood to mean that two researchers are not of equal status, with one being more senior, powerful, or more persuasive than the other. In this scenario, it could lead to the more powerful or persuasive researcher unduly influencing the other person to act in a certain way that compromises them. It can occur in institutions where one researcher persuades another researcher not to speak up about perceived breaches. Again, status asymmetries are a fact of work life, but they can be managed. Researchers need to use common sense in making decisions and stand firm when another researcher tries to unduly influence them to breach ethical principles.
3. 'Publish or perish' is a catch phrase that everyone in universities or research institutes understands. *Researchers are required to produce a volume of research annually.* They are evaluated on that research output as part of the requirements in an increasingly competitive research environment. Researchers may feel the pressure to produce quality articles in highly ranked journals or to win grants from national government agencies in order to remain relevant. Furthermore, rapid changes in the arts and cultural management discipline mean that ethical guidelines, drafted according to the needs of other disciplines such as medicine, have to change to "fit the mold." Researchers need to be alert to such pressures when undertaking projects.

Ethical breaches can occur on a spectrum from minor to major, simple to complex, or anywhere in between if investigated or audited. For example, ethical breaches are not only found in traditional places but also in contemporary challenges to ancient dreamtime issues, such as how to undertake

First Nations research (e.g. see Rentschler et al., 2020). In such circumstances, ethical breaches are assessed according to:

1. The origin of the research breach (i.e., the researcher; the institution)
2. The seniority and experience of the researcher (i.e., junior versus senior researcher)
3. The scope and severity of the breach (i.e., impact on the authenticity and legitimacy of the project; isolated instance or recurrent behaviour; consequences of the breach to individuals and community) (Drolet et al., 2023)

Ethical breaches can cause distress to individual researchers, reputational damage to academic institutions, and disrespect to individuals and communities who are the subject of the research project. It is not always easy for investigators to examine a potential breach, as they need to understand the discipline, the research approach, and/or have the depth and breadth of experience to engage with the study. Some breaches are technical slips or mistakes, which have no impact on the project authenticity and legitimacy. Other breaches are more serious, with widespread impact on the veracity of the data, the findings of the study, the researcher, and/or the institution and the community.

A research ethics framework

Researchers in the social sciences, such as in arts and cultural management, need a research ethics framework. Figure 3.1 illustrates a research ethics framework that is applicable for an arts and cultural research study. It shows the seven steps in the process that might occur during a study. It also shows the importance of respect, trust, and being accountable and responsible to the effective working of the framework.

A research ethics framework is important because many countries and most universities have codes of ethics that govern how research studies are undertaken. For example, the Australian code for the responsible conduct of research (*The Code*, 2023) provides an example of a code of ethics at the national level that is used in all Australian universities and research institutes. The code outlines four values for researchers to follow in the conduct of their research:

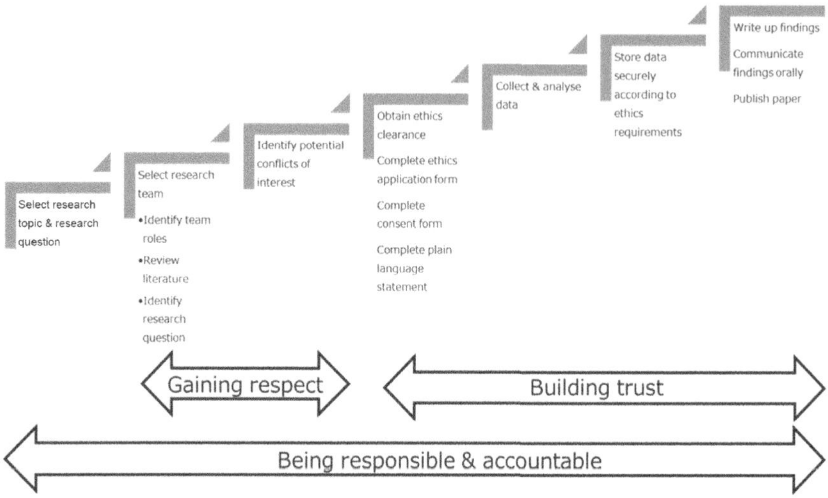

Figure 3.1 Steps in ethical research process

1. *Research merit and integrity:* Research that is justified because of its potential benefit and contribution to knowledge, using appropriate methods with researchers who are trained and skilled to undertake it
2. *Justice:* Research that selects inclusion or exclusion of participants through fair means, accurately describing results
3. *Beneficence:* Research that benefits the participants, the wider community or both
4. *Respect:* Research that treats participants with respect for their individuality, confidentiality, community, customs and beliefs, privacy and confidentiality.

(*The Code*, 2023, pp. 10–11)

Codes of ethics were developed with good intent in the various nations in which they operate. However, sometimes, official systems, such as how to gain approval for research – designed to prevent a repetition of a shameful history – can prove bureaucratic and inflexible (Martino & Schormans, 2018; Slowther, Boynton & Shaw, 2006; Smith, 2021). The Australian Code for the Responsible Conduct of Research, (2018) has been revised recently to take into account such criticisms. Bureaucracy can damage the good intent of those who developed codes of ethics. Hence, it is important that codes of ethics remain current as the field changes rapidly. Further, discussion of research governance and ethical conduct remains fragmented across nations, with guidelines sometimes patchy. This is despite the prevalence of core ethical principles across codes of ethics, such as respect for autonomy, prevention of harm, benefit to participants, and justice. Such codes need to be communicated widely, applied flexibly and with common sense to take account of community differences, contextual, methodological, personal, and practical considerations. Ensuring that the design and conduct of research is sound is the responsibility of everyone undertaking research – researchers, research institutions, ethics committees, and regulatory bodies (Slowther, Boynton & Shaw, 2006; Tsimas & Demetriades, 2021) – and the communities researchers serve.

Despite numerous challenges, all pieces of the research puzzle, from start to finish, need to be trustworthy and to earn the respect of participants in the study (Bassey & Owen, 2019). Guidelines are devised to ensure that research studies are well-planned processes that examine phenomena using appropriate tools for data gathering, analysis, and communication. Now let's look at the steps in the research ethics process in Figure 3.1.

Steps in the research ethics process

As introduced at the beginning of this chapter, the ethical process rarely proceeds in a linear or orderly manner. Research is a messy business, but it is written up as if it were tidy. Nonetheless, it is useful to visualize the ethical process in a research project as an idealized framework for discussion. Such an ethical process is useful when planning roles and responsibilities of researchers in the project. Each of the seven steps is now explained.

1. *Select research topic and research question* The research topic and research question for a particular research project allow the researcher to establish the aim, scope, approach, and the focus of the study. These matters are further refined when undertaking the literature search and review processes. It is at this stage in the research process that you ask yourself WHY you are undertaking this study.
2. *Select research team* A research project can be undertaken by one researcher or a team of researchers, from small to large, in one institution, one country, or across a range of institutions and countries. The size and type of research team depends on the purpose of the

research project and the question to be answered. It is in step 2 that you ask yourself WHAT personnel you need to ensure the study is going to be a success. Once the team is in place, you can conduct a literature search and review, concluding with deciding the research question.

3. *Identify potential conflicts of interest* In this step, the researcher asks themselves if they can identify any perceived or actual conflicts of interest that need to be managed. Some researchers write a list of conflicts of interest that may arise and how they intend to handle them to ensure they do not derail the study.
4. *Obtain ethics clearance* Step 4 entails applying for ethics clearance for your study. Having identified the aim, scope, and focus of your study, conducted the literature search and determined a research question, and the sensitivities you perceive may be entailed in it will guide you as to what type of ethics clearance to obtain. Most ethics processes also require you to complete a consent form and a plain language statement.
5. *Collect and analyze data* With ethics approval obtained, you can start collecting and analyzing data.
6. *Store data securely according to requirements* When you apply for ethical clearance for your study, you will be required to identify HOW and WHERE you will store your data, how long you will keep the data and WHO will have access to it. Normally, it is only the immediate research team that has access to the data.
7. *Write up, publish, and communicate findings* An important final step in the framework is writing up your study, publishing the findings, and communicating the findings to stakeholders. Deciding WHEN to communicate findings is also important, as it is a means of building trust and respect among participants. Communication can entail presentation at academic or industry conferences and or providing participants with a summary of findings or a short presentation on them. It is considered courteous to share the findings with participants as a means of thanking them for their time and insights.

The rest of the framework illustrates the three key ethical research principles of gaining respect, building trust, and being responsible and accountable.

Gaining respect

Gaining respect entails giving participants the autonomy to make a decision as to whether or not to participate in a study and whether or not to provide informed consent. Informed consent is defined as granting permission in full knowledge of the benefits and risks of participating in the study. Informed consent forms usually can be obtained simply by participating in the study, by orally agreeing to participate in the study, or by stating in writing that they agree to participate in the study. Given the wide scope of what informed consent means, it is prudent to record it in some form.

There are additional challenges in collecting qualitative data for research studies (Parry & Mauthner, 2004). In quantitative studies, and indeed in most ethical guidelines, respect is considered straightforward as it is generally considered that by undertaking a survey, for example, the participant is giving consent. In qualitative studies, undertaking the study is a joint endeavor between the participant and the researcher. The joint construction of qualitative data which is "owned" by researcher and participants in the study makes gaining respect anything but straightforward.

If data are jointly created in qualitative studies, then it is reasonable to assume that access to that data should not be obtained without the approval of both the researcher and the participant and sometimes the community. It also complicates the notion of informed consent. Informed consent is assumed to be a straightforward matter (according to a positivist paradigm) of seeking approval (in writing or by other means) from participants. But for some qualitative studies, approval is more than a piece of paper. It is about being respected as a person first and then second form-filling as a lower-order process or sometimes even a feared process (Cook, 2023). Overcoming that fear is done by gaining participant respect first and considering monitoring activities later in the process.

However, institutional ethical guidelines sometimes overlook such complexities, despite calls for their review (McGaw & Vance, 2023). They can be written from a positivist, quantitative perspective without considering the needs of joint endeavors in qualitative studies. For example, there have been calls not to allow access to data to outside parties unless it has been approved by the participant (Parry & Mauthner, 2004). However, such complex ethical issues have yet to be resolved satisfactorily. Nonetheless, they are important for researchers to consider before undertaking their study.

Building trust

Today, the definition of trust is broader than it was traditionally. Now, ethical conduct includes building trust through behavior toward participants that entails research integrity, avoiding or managing conflicts of interest, providing benefits to participants in the research process while protecting them and their communities from harm, as well as the traditional term of fabrication, falsification, and plagiarism. Building trust takes time.

At the simplest level, a research methodology builds trust through its two aims: (i) to develop data from participants; and (ii) to represent their world view authentically (Cook, 2023). In developing data, there are questions about whom to trust, why, and when, with a bias to trusting gatekeepers, such as examiners or journal editors, rather than the participants from whom data are collected (Cook, 2023).

Behaving well when making decisions about the research process is what building trust entails. It ensures research integrity includes building trust with participants and communities to be studied (Kopec, 2023; Yin, 2011). Building trust is encoded in ethical standards or guiding principles promoted by professional bodies and universities. Ethical standards are available online and contain guidelines for research conduct and the importance of building trust with the community who participates in research projects. For example, the Australian National Human Research Ethics code of conduct states:

> All human interaction, including the interaction involved in human research, has ethical dimensions. However, 'ethical conduct' is more than simply doing the right thing. It involves acting in the right spirit, out of an abiding respect and concern for one's fellow creatures. The National Statement on 'ethical conduct in human research' is therefore oriented to something more fundamental than ethical 'do's' and 'don'ts' – namely, an ethos that should permeate the way those engaged in human research approach all that they do in their research.
>
> Human research is research conducted with or about people . . .
>
> First, research participants may enter into a relationship with researchers whom they may not know but need to trust. This trust adds to the ethical responsibility borne by those in whom it is placed. Secondly, many who contribute as participants in human research do so altruistically, for the common good, without thought

> of recompense for their time and effort. This underscores the importance of protecting research participants.
>
> (*The Code*, 2023, p. 4)

The principle of trust is universal: it concerns empowering individuals engaged in the research as much as building relationships with participants, so that they benefit from the research. In more and more countries, studies about people need ethics approval from an institutional ethics committee (Yin, 2011), which is seen as a proxy for trust. In most cases, ethics approval helps build trust with participants to know that a research institution backs your research project. However, there are instances where some participants distrust bureaucracy and thus the ethics process, such as some minority groups (e.g., see Cook, 2023; McGaw & Vance, 2023; Parry & O'Mauther, 2004). Hence, in some instances, building trust can occur independently of ethics processes but may still be necessary from a country and institutional perspective.

Being responsible and accountable

Further to the scenario sketched at the beginning of this chapter, it has been shown that responsibility and accountability for research governance and ethical conduct need to be flexible and inclusive of differing social contexts in which research projects are undertaken (Mavhandu-Mudzusi, 2023). While there may be no agreement to some of the ethical dilemmas surrounding research governance and ethical conduct, codified behavior has seen the development of norms of conduct that guide our research. These norms are the shared responsibility of the individual researcher or research team, the research community of influence or interest in and for the project (potentially a funding agency if the research project received funding, or if there is no funding, it may simply be the community who will benefit from the project), and the research institution, such as a university. This section provides a brief overview of the varying responsibilities and accountabilities of each of these parties in the research project and process.

Individual

Translating ethical principles into the specific context of individual research projects in different social and cultural settings can pose challenges for researchers, ethics review committees, and regulatory bodies. Concepts such as informed consent are open to interpretation and influence within specific social and political contexts. For example, in France, legal and ethical guidelines are less restrictive than in other European countries or Australia in relation to studies with participants who lack ability to make an informed choice as to whether or not to take part in the study, reflecting different cultural traditions. Nonetheless, the individual researcher needs to ensure that they have obtained informed consent from study participants. Normally, this entails asking participants if they will participate, and often having participants sign a consent form, and an information sheet explaining the project in plain language.

A consent form may be a written document in hard copy or an online version of consent that is recorded when data are gathered. Given consent is then able to be kept as a record that provides evidence of approval to undertake the study with that individual or group. Consent can be simply obtained by using following words at the beginning of the data collection process:

> **Consent for interview**
> I give consent for you to undertake this interview. I understand the purpose of the study and my role in it. I understand participation is voluntary and I can withdraw from the study at any time. I agree to the interview being recorded. I agree to anonymous quotes being used in publications that may arise from the study.
>
> **Consent for online survey**
> I understand that by undertaking this survey I am giving consent to participate in this study. I understand participation is voluntary and I can withdraw from the study at any time. I agree to aggregated data being used in publications that may arise from the study.

As with other areas of research governance and ethical conduct, there are some gray areas. Obtaining consent for observations can sometimes be tricky. If observations are undertaken, for example, in a boardroom, then consent can be obtained from the organization and the individuals participating in the board meeting. However, if the researcher wishes to observe audience behavior in a theater or at a festival, it is almost impossible to obtain consent from everyone present. The way some researchers get around this gray area is to have a QR code placed on the screen at the front of the theatre to which participants can link if they wish to participate or, in a simple and traditional manner, place a notice at the entry to the theatre or festival, advising participants that observations may take place at this event, with contact details of the researcher(s). If participants do not wish to be part of the study, they simply do not click on the QR code or they advise the researcher. Similar processes are followed for photography, filming, or streaming of arts events. Some scholars consider ethics approval necessary for gray areas of research, but form-filling unnecessary for such activities (Veal & Burton, 2015). If that were to be the case, then the matter of anonymity in reporting findings of the study becomes even more critical.

The purpose of an information sheet is to explain the purpose of the study. The information sheet uses easy-to-understand language. It usually contains the following:

- Title of the study
- Names of researchers and research institution
- Purpose of the study and its benefit to the participants and or to the community
- Activities required if they participate
- Amount of time taken by participation
- Any risks in participating
- Rights to withdraw at any time in the study
- Participant anonymity
- Where, for how long, and how data will be stored
- Those who have access to the data (i.e., the research team)

The purpose of a consent form is to have a record of consent in case it is required by the research institution, the participant, or due to an audit function of the research process being undertaken. The consent form usually contains information drawn from the information sheet and summarized in one page. It is usually signed by the participant and the researcher (Olson, 2011). The purpose of the information sheet is to provide participants with a brief overview of the study, so that they know what they are agreeing to.

Assignment of authorship to publications becomes an ethical issue when authorship is inappropriately allocated to a scholar who has not contributed to the work adequately. It is also an ethical issue when authorship is not awarded to those that have contributed to the work (Mumford et al., 2010). Authorship needs to be discussed and agreed upon at the beginning of a project and recorded in writing. It also needs to be revisited during the project, as contributions to the project can change over time. Any changes to authorship can then be recorded.

Community

The meaning of the word 'ethics' underlines its philosophical and controversial nature. It comes from the Greek word 'ethos,' meaning a community's shared customs or an individual's character, whether good or bad, and with shades of meaning in between (Booth, Columb & Williams, 2008).

It is important to respect the individual researcher as well as the individual participant in the study, plus their community, whether it be a virtual or real community (Liu et al, 2025a and b; Guest editorial, 2020; Walmsley, 2019). Such respect recognizes the differences in ways of conducting research in Western or other contexts. Researchers should review community practices before going into the field, to ensure they gain the trust of participants and their community, thus avoiding any embarrassing cross-cultural misunderstandings. If the researcher is dealing with people in abject poverty, then beneficence supersedes 'harm' discussed in most ethics policies with a developed Western world focus (Mavhandu-Mudzusi, 2023). It requires more flexibility in research ethics than may be the norm.

Institutional

Institutional responsibility and accountability for research governance entails developing policy that recognizes and responds to the ethical dimensions of the research process (Slowther, Boynton & Shaw, 2006), so that academics are aware of their individual responsibility and accountability in research governance and ethical conduct. Nations and research institutions, such as universities, develop ethical regulatory frameworks and codes of ethics to reflect the need to understand potential ethical risks in undertaking research. After establishing policies, institutions are responsible for promulgating the content of those policies and providing induction, training, and mentors for academics that reinforce the behaviors expected in undertaking research projects. Providing a supportive institutional framework is essential to enable individual academics to be effective in carrying out research projects in an ethical manner.

Table 3.1 illustrates the principles, policy, and praxis in research governance and ethical conduct. It outlines the key principles discussed in this

Table 3.1 Research governance and ethical conduct: Principles, policy and praxis

Principles	Policy	Praxis	Questions
Trust	National and institutional policy guidelines on research governance and ethical conduct Induction of new academics provided in research governance and ethical conduct Mentor research governance and ethical conduct provided to new academics Ongoing training and professional development provided to academics in research governance and ethical conduct	Institutional ethics approval Participant consent obtained Conflicts of interest discussed and resolved	*Research team:* Has the research team obtained institutional human research ethics approval for the research project? Has the research team allocated roles and responsibilities? Has the research team discussed and resolved any potential conflicts of interest? *Individual researcher:* Have I built a relationship of trust with participants? Have I obtained consent from participants for participating in the research project, and if so, how?
Respect		Minimize harm and maximize participant and or community benefit (Mavhundu-Mudzuhsi, 2023) Understand power differentials between researcher, participants, and community (Drolet et al., 2023; Mavhundu-Mudzuhsi, 2023) Authentically represent a world view (Cook, 2023) Authentically report others' ideas in publications (The Code, 2023)	*Research team:* Has the research team taken care to authentically report data from the study to various audiences and in various formats? *Individual researcher:* Have I operated with respect for participants throughout the project? Have I ensured that participants and the community benefit from the study?

(*Continued*)

Table 3.1 (*Continued*)

Principles	Policy	Praxis	Questions
Institutional ethical responsibility		Ethical support and guidance (Drolet et al., 2023) through: • induction for new researchers • training and mentoring for researchers Recognize culture of individualism in Western research institutions; ethical bureaucracy versus need for trust and respect for participants and communities; ethical issues in qualitative projects is sometimes devalued (Drolet et al., 2023)	*Research institution:* Does my institution provide induction, mentoring and training in research governance and ethical conduct? *Research team:* Has the research team considered the bias against qualitative research in some research institutional settings? *Individual researcher:* Have I taken the opportunity to partake in induction, training, and mentoring throughout my academic career to continue to learn about research governance and ethical conduct?
Individual ethical responsibility		Records of data, why, when, and where collected, by whom, with online links to data storage	*Research team:* Has the research team allocated one team member to be responsible for data management for the research project? Has the research team kept a record of the data collected, how, by whom, when, and where?
Community ethical responsibility		Balance individual, institutional, and community norms in research (Drolet et al., 2023)	*Research team:* Has the research team selected a research paradigm and world view and articulated it clearly in the study? Has the research team discussed and resolved the greater focus in Western nations on the individual rather than the community benefit of research projects?

chapter: trust, respect, institutional ethical responsibility, individual ethical responsibility, and community ethical responsibility. It then provides a brief overview of the national and institutional policy initiatives that frame research governance and ethical conduct. Next, it provides a summary of what happens in praxis in research governance and ethical conduct. Finally, the last column in the table provides prompt questions for the individual researcher or the research team to ask themselves as they go about their study.

Conclusion

In this chapter, the challenges of research governance and ethical conduct were introduced. As seen in the scenarios, some cases are clear-cut while others are controversial. The three parties to the research process – researcher, participant and/or their community, and research institution – examined in this chapter all have roles, responsibilities, and accountabilities. The research institution provides the codified guidelines or the philosophical framework for undertaking ethical research, often within a country framework. It also provides training, professional development, and mentoring to academic researchers. The researchers themselves adhere to the purpose of the research project, obtain ethical approval to undertake the study and comply with the guidelines for doing so, develop trust and maintain confidentiality of participants (where necessary), maintain records of the research process and records of the data collected and analyzed, and represent the findings of the study appropriately. The participants and/or their community see the benefits of the research or indeed, in some instances, the harm it has done them. They avoid misrepresenting the findings to others.

References

Alvesson, M., & Stephens, A. (2024), "'Is it worth doing this or is it better to commit suicide?' ON ethical clearance at a university," *Human Relations*, 1–30.

Bassey, B. A., & Owan, V. J. (2019), "Ethical issues in educational research management and practice," in P. N. Ololube, & G. U. Nwiyi (Eds.), *Encyclopedia of institutional leadership, policy, and management: A handbook of research in honour of Professor Ozo-Mekuri Ndimele* (pp. 1287–1301). Port Harcourt, NG: Pearl Publishers International Ltd.

Booth, W. C., Colomb, G. G., & Williams, J. M. (2008), "The ethics of research," in *The craft of research* (pp. 273–276). The University of Chicago Press.

Cook, P. (2023), "Talk-story: Performing an indigenous research methodology with hesitant non-indigenous participants to learn previously silenced knowledge," *International Journal of Qualitative Methods*, 22, 1–11.

Drolet, M., Rose-Derouin, E., Leblanc, J., Ruest, M., & Williams-Jones, B. (2023), "Ethical issues in research: Perceptions of researchers, research ethics board members and research ethics experts," *Journal of Academic Ethics*, 21, 269–292.

Guest Editorial. (2020), "Guest editorial: Ethical issues in social media research," *Journal of Empirical Research on Human Research Ethics*, 15(1–2), 3–11, special issue on Social Media Research Ethics.

Kopec, A. (2023), "Policy feedback & research methods: How qualitative research designs with marginalized groups inform theory," *International Journal of Qualitative Methods*, 22, 1–12.

Liu, J., Lee, B., & Rentschler, R. (2025a), "Are art investors rational? Investor sentiments and art returns," in E. Lazzaro, N. Moureau, & A. Turpin (Eds.), *Law and finance in international art markets: Past and present*. Routledge.

Liu, J., Lee, B., & Rentschler, R. (2025b), "Leveraging entrepreneurial identity and technology: Legitimacy of art securitization platforms," *Journal of Cultural Economics*, special issue on Art, Technology and Entrepreneurship.

Martino, A. S., & Schormans, A. F. (2018), "When go good intentions backfire: University research ethics review and the intimate lives of people labelled with intellectual disabilities," *Foruam Qualitative Sozialforschung/Forum: Qualitative Social Research*, 19(3). http://doi.org/10/17169/fqs-19,3.3090.

Mavhandu-Mudzusi, A. H. (2023), "Application of ethics in the South African rural context," *International Journal of Qualitative Methods*, 22, 1–9.

McGaw, J., & Vance, A. (2023), "Dissonance, disagreement, difference: Challenging thematic consensus to decolonise grounded theory," *International Journal of Qualitative Methods*, 22, 1–12.

Mumford, M. D., Waples, E. P., Antes, A. L., Brown, R. P., Connelly, S., Murphy, S. T., & Devenport, L. D. (2010), "Creativity and ethics: The relationship of creative and ethical problem-solving," *Creativity Research Journal*, 22(1), 74–89.

National Statement on Human Conduct in Ethical Research. (2023), *The Code National Health and Medical Research Council, Australian Research Council and Universities Australia*. Commonwealth of Australia, Canberra.

Olson, K. (2011), "Ethical issues in interviewing," in K. Olson (Ed.), *Essentials of qualitative interviewing*. Walnut Creek: Left Coast Press.

Parry, O., & Mauthner, N. S. (2004), "Whose data are they anyway? Practical, legal and ethical issues in archiving qualitative data," *Sociology*, 38(1), 139–152.

Rentschler, R., Belk, R., Hawkes, M., & Martin, B. (2020), "'I am the old and the new': Aboriginal arts in the Australian art world 1972–2018," *Journal of Business Diversity*, 20(2), 74–93.

Rentschler, R., Lee, B., & Subramaniam, N. (2021), "Calculative practices and socio-political tensions: A historical analysis of entertainment, arts and accounting in a government agency," *Accounting History*, 26(1), 80–101.

Slowther, A., Boynton, P., & Shaw, S. (2006), "Research governance: Ethical issues," *Journal of the Royal Society of Medicine*, 99, 65–72.

Smith, L. T. (2021), *Decolonizing methodologies: Research and indigenous peoples* (3rd ed.). Zed Books.

Tzimas, D., & Demetriadis, S. (2021), "Ethical issues in learning analytics: A review of the field," *Education Technology Research and Development*, 69, 1101–1133.

Veal, A. J., & Burton, C. (2015), *Research methods for arts and event management*. UTS Faculty of Business. http://hdl.handle.net/10453/35442.

Walmsley, B. (2019), *Audience engagement in the performing arts: A critical analysis*. Cham: Palgrave Macmillan.

Winter, R., & Lavis, A. (2020), "Looking, lurking but not listening? Theorising the ethics of listening in online ethnographic research," *Journal of Empirical Research on Human Research Ethics*, 15(1–2), 55–62, special issue on Social Media Research Ethics.

Yin, R. (2011), "Setting and maintaining ethical standards of conduct," in *Qualitative research from start to finish* (pp. 38–48). New York: The Guildford Press.

Zigmund, W. G. (1994), "Ethical issues in business research," in *Business research methods* (International ed., 4th ed., p. 54). Fort Worth: The Dryden Press.

4

WHAT, WHY, AND HOW

WRITING A LITERATURE REVIEW

Introduction

A good place to start is by defining a literature review. A literature review has no single accepted definition. However, a good rule of thumb is that a literature review comprises a comprehensive overview of prior studies on a particular topic. It is a critical component of any study that entails summarizing and synthesizing that literature to provide the reader with a systematic or thematic account of what has been published, stating what is known and what is unknown about the present study, and why filling a gap is important to the study. The literature review provides a *rationale* for the study by identifying the gap in prior research that the study fills (Hart, 2018).

The next step is to consider the type of literature review you wish to undertake for your research study. There are numerous different types of literature review. In this chapter, we consider three of them in more detail: a thematic literature review (Bürger & Volkmann, 2020; Rentschler & Liu, 2024), a systematic literature review (Colbert et al., 2023; Simonnot-Lanciaux et al., 2025), and an annotated bibliographic analysis (Ferreira, 2018; Noonan, 2002). A thematic literature review is self-explanatory: as you read, you identify themes in the literature and structure your literature review around a few key themes. A systematic literature review is an integrated review which examines prior literature and the approaches taken in the studies, helping you to identify the gaps in the literature that will guide your study and how it will

DOI: 10.4324/9781003487951-4

fill them. An annotated bibliographic analysis is a process of providing the bibliographic citation to prior works of literature and devising a summary of each work. For the emerging scholar, it is more a tool taken on the journey to creating a literature review of the first or second types. Indeed, sometimes literature reviews include more than one approach in the one study (e.g., see Casadei et al., 2023, who use both a bibliometric and thematic analysis; see also Simonnot-Lanciaux et al., 2025, who use systematic, bibliographic, and spectroscopy analysis).

Having examined three popular types of literature review, we briefly explain some of the emergent types of literature reviews in arts and cultural management. Some of them are qualitative (e.g., netnography), others quantitative (e.g., spectroscopy; meta-analysis), or indeed sometimes a mix of the two or more types in the one publication.

However, let's start by examining what a literature review entails and then provide a brief overview of common steps in a literature review. The rest of the chapter proceeds with explaining the types of literature review, before the conclusion.

What is a literature review?

A scholar faced with the task of writing a literature review may feel at a loss and wonder where to start it. Do not panic. There is more often than not an extensive prior literature in the domain in which you wish to undertake your study.

Here are some questions a student starting their career in research may ask:

> How important is a literature review when it comes to conducting research? What is the difference between a literature review, needed in the case of writing an article, and a synthesis of an entire body of the literature on a given subject? What do I need to know, and are there different types of literature reviews?

In answering these questions, it might be helpful to visualize the place of the literature review in the research process. Figure 4.1 shows that the literature review starts broadly, from the context of the arts and cultural management field, then narrows to arts audiences, and finally focuses on audience engagement, a sliver of arts marketing. It illustrates the literature review as

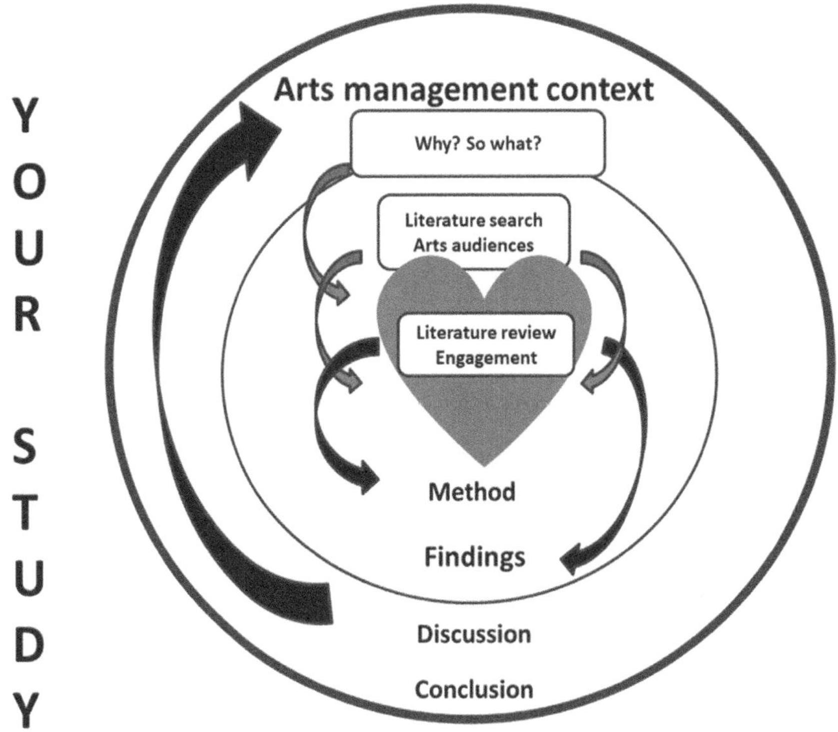

Figure 4.1 The literature review: The heart of the study

a series of concentric circles, asking broad, open questions until it helps to refine the research question for your study and eventually has your question answered in the findings, and then enriches the literature in the discussion and conclusion of your study. But it doesn't end there. The literature review you have undertaken then loops back to the beginning, providing insights for future studies, making it a dynamic process (Rentschler & Liu (2024). As you can see in Figure 4.1, the literature review is at the heart of your research. It affects everything else that you do in your study.

As was mentioned before, you must find in what conversation you want to participate in. In order to find this, you must look to what others before you have published. Embarking on data collection without this preliminary step runs the risk of your work reinventing the wheel, i.e., someone before you has already published an article on exactly your problem, or interesting results obtained by other researchers could have better oriented you so as to maximize your chances of producing results that add relevant knowl-

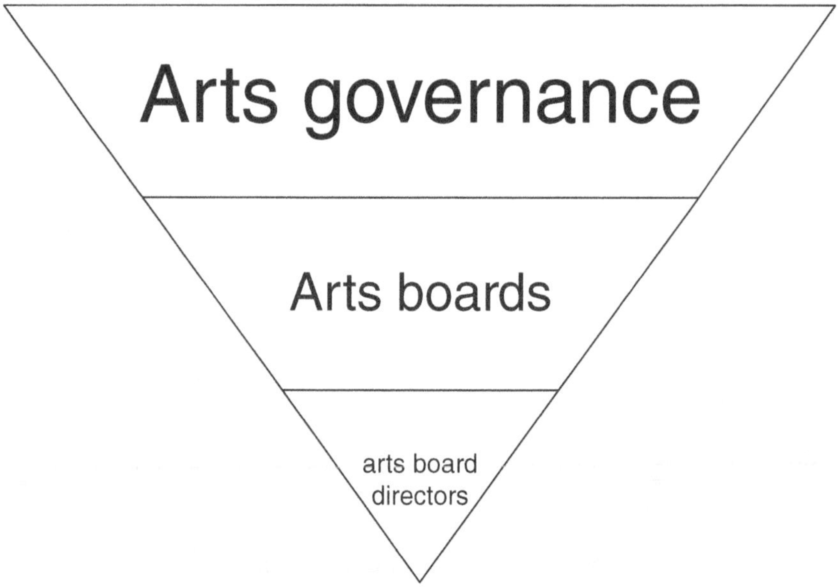

Figure 4.2 Literature review: From broad to narrow

edge to the literature. This is all the more important when you are thinking of submitting the results of your work to a scientific journal. Because not only will the thesis or dissertation supervisor want the candidate to have done this groundwork, but the anonymous reviewers of the targeted journal will also want to know where your research stands in the body of scientific knowledge.

Steps in your literature review process

What you are trying to do in this preliminary stage is to define the playing field, in order to provide boundaries within which you are going to devote your efforts. To illustrate the concept, think of an inverted triangle (Figure 4.2), where each level of the triangle, from top to bottom, shows how the literature review moves from broad to narrow. Your study will not examine the whole field, but a slice of it that is under-researched, but deep and narrow in scope. Figure 4.2 visualizes how you move from broadly what is known to what is unknown as your literature review advances. Prior literature may not all be in arts and cultural management. If you are studying arts governance, you may need to start by looking further afield, in the corporate governance and nonprofit governance literature, and then narrow down the search to the arts and cultural domain.

The triangle provides the boundaries and the bottom part identifying the gap you choose to investigate. Or said differently, you will ask yourself: Where is the gap in the literature? What will the study's contribution to the extant literature be? Remember that you live or die by your contribution. An important contribution to new knowledge boosts your standing as a scholar, and a publisher will want to publish the work. On the other hand, if the contribution is a minor one, you may find yourself facing difficulty in finding a journal to publish your work. The same can be said of your thesis committee if the contribution to new knowledge is not clearly articulated.

The following example shows how to illustrate the gap in the literature that your study has identified (Simonnot et al., 2025, p. 43):

> The quantitative method named "Reference Publication Year Spectroscopy" (RPYS) (allows you to) determine the historical roots of research fields and quantify their impact on current *isolated phenomena, or the historical development of the music industry. However, a comprehensive understanding of the development and evolution of music marketing research itself is lacking. This study addresses this gap by examining how music marketing research has emerged and changed over time.*

As we can see, with this simple example, the authors inform us of the gaps in the literature they propose to fill.

Once you have defined the knowledge gap, you are in a position to state your research question, which guides you through the next steps in the study. In the case of quantitative research, you will have both research questions and research hypotheses. In the case of qualitative research, you will have an overarching research question and may also have propositions. The steps in the literature review process are as follows:

1. Define the constructs or concepts you are going to use

It can happen that different authors give a slightly different definition of a concept. In the case several definitions have been proposed, it is wise to state in the introduction which definition of the concept or construct you are going to use. You can give your reasons in the "literature review" section, mentioning the main definitions you have found. Whatever definition you choose – and this depends on your research objective – the important thing is that the reader knows what to expect.

2. *Explain your contribution to new knowledge*

One of the main reasons for a study to be rejected by a journal is its lack of contribution to new knowledge, a weak contribution, or an unclear contribution (Ladik & Stewart, 2008). The rest of the study may be of high quality, flawless research design, rigorous analysis, but if it makes no new contribution to knowledge, the study may be rejected. So, what you need to do is explain why your study is important and worthy of publication, how it extends theory, and how it adds something new to the body of knowledge. The more your study makes a substantial theoretical contribution, and the more it helps to solve a problem that the academic community considers important, the greater your chances of publication. Having said that, avoid listing all contributions. Concentrate on your major contribution, or a very limited number of major contributions. If your contribution is also managerial, mention it if it is appropriate for the journal you are targeting. For an interesting reading on "contribution," please refer to Ladik and Stewart (2008) in which they explain and illustrate different types of contributions (see also Chapter 2).

One common mistake made by emerging researchers is to state the contribution too broadly. Broad statements, such as nobody has published on that subject in that industry, are too indistinct. Statements need to be linked to prior research and theory specifically. It is rarely sufficient. If no work has been undertaken on a particular aspect of a topic, it may be due to its insignificance or unimportance to the field. Be careful to choose a problem that makes a difference to the field.

3. *Address your audience*

Again, you need to remember that a study is a discussion between the author, the publisher, the reviewers, and ultimately the community you seek to engage. An academic audience seeks to know how your study adds to the knowledge base of the field. A practitioner audience wants to know how to apply your research findings in practice. If reviewers provide mixed reviews about your paper's contribution, the editor will decide whether or not to publish it. Reviewers evaluate your study as a piece of work in itself. The editor may decide to publish it because they find something interesting in your study. They evaluate it in relation to other considerations. If the study has no major flaws and they are convinced it is worthy of publication, they may accept it, while making comments to the author in such a way as to solidify it. Always remember, it is up to you to ensure that the contribution is stated clearly. It is up to you to persuade the reviewers and the editor that your study deserves to be published in their journal.

This last remark raises another important point. The author needs to ensure that the journal targeted for publication of the study accepts the type of research carried out. For example, some journals do not publish qualitative research, so there is no point in submitting your qualitative work to them. Likewise, each journal publishes an "Author's Guide" which, as its name suggests, outlines for the author how the manuscript is to be presented, including, for example, how to format references. It is important to decide early on which journal to submit the study to (ideally, at the very beginning of the research project). In this way, you can better anticipate key elements to be taken into account when writing the manuscript for publication, and focus, structure, and revise it accordingly.

Types of literature review

Apart from a literature review for a thesis or academic article, there is a form of literature review, the objective of which is to find gaps, inconsistencies, or other aspects of the scientific knowledge that need analyzing in the entire or a major part of a body of literature. But before we do so, let's look at some basic principles important to one who wants to undertake a literature review as their main area of research.

It is useful for the research community to have access to works that take stock of a phenomenon and propose avenues for research. In this type of research, we are interested both in what we know about a phenomenon and in what we do not know. This leads us to think about 'why we don't know more, and how other researchers have thought about parts of the question.' It's not enough to structure and describe what we know. We also need – and this is an important part – to think about avenues of research that might take knowledge further. In doing so, we need to have a defined purpose. As the aim of our work is not generally to explore the whole field of knowledge, we need to specify from the outset what we are trying to do. This is the equivalent of identifying the gap in a research article and marking out the boundaries.

However, one must show how important the work is and how we intend to accomplish it. As Paré, Wagner and Prester (2023, p. 3) wrote:

> A common pitfall observed in many submissions involves providing insufficient justification for the importance of the topic and research questions, and for how the review article contributed new knowledge.

Through the following example, let see how an author has positioned their comprehensive literature review:

> This paper provides a comprehensive literature review of empirical studies of motion picture performance published from 1977 to 2006 inclusive in the following five disciplines of the social sciences: strategy, organization theory, marketing, cultural economics and sociology. It introduces a novel framework which organizes the various dimensions and explanatory factors of movie performance into five distinct categories and underscores their relationships. The paper, which uses this model as a roadmap for discussions of film success, serves two complementary purposes. First, it clarifies the current state of the literature, stresses core contributions and exposes limitations in existing research by emphasizing hitherto neglected independent explanatory factors, dependent dimensions and correlations between them. Second, it introduces five conceptual, methodological and empirical suggestions for further cinema performance research aimed at addressing these limitations and, accordingly, at providing better accounts of motion picture performance in view of the fast-changing conditions of cinema production, marketing and consumption.
>
> (Hadida, 2009, p. 297)

Such a literature review is useful for researchers since it points to lack of or inconsistency in the current knowledge about film and proposes an agenda for future research.

Before talking more about types of literature reviews, let us remind ourselves that the characteristics of a good literature review are to be concise, clear, critical, convincing, and contributive (Callahan, 2014); concise means what it means; clear imposes that you script clearly the method you used to appraise the literature; critical brings you to be critical in your reflection and analysis of the literature; convincing will present the reader with a convincing argument why your research is needed; and contributive, meaning how you add to the existing knowledge. Readers interested in learning more about the subject could read in particular Pickering and Byrne (2014), Whittemore and Knafl (2005), Kennedy (2007), or Torraco (2005).

1. Thematic literature review

The thematic literature review enables you to situate your research thematically by what is known and what is yet to be known in the aspect of your field that you are investigating. It also enables you to articulate your scholarly approach, justify the importance of your subject, and show how it adds something new to the body of knowledge. In other words, it provides your study with trustworthiness and authenticity as well as credibility. A well-crafted and interesting thematic literature review makes the reader want to look further, boosts your credibility as a researcher, positions your study thematically in relation to prior literature, and identifies gaps and how they have been filled by the thematic literature review undertaken.

A thematic literature review is not an opportunity to include everything that you've read. When you've put a lot of effort into researching, reading, and assimilating the content of a large body of knowledge, the tendency is to want to use everything you've read. Resist this very human reaction. First of all, you need to sort through the publications you've found. Keep only those that support you in answering your research question, your world view, and scholarly approach, as well as those that are the most important, and those that will enable you to better define your research topic. You'll need to cite both classic publications and more recent works. You don't need to summarize each publication article by article. Publications should be grouped by themes or sub-themes, so as to highlight the main thrust of your study. Here's an example from an article by Euzéby, Passebois-Ducros and Machat (2024, p. 21)

> Hence, Internet users judge the credibility of the publication from peripheral cues such as photo quality, the style or quality of the writing (Xiao, Wang & Chan-Olmsted, 2018). Social cues (the

> number of likes, views, of followers) also play a key role in judgments of messages and sources.
>
> (Hu & Yao, 2022; Fogg et al., 2003; Metzger, Flanagin & Medders, 2010)

As you can see, the authors haven't summarized the articles but presented a synthesis of subject themes and referred the reader to the authors who provide evidence in support of their argument.

Another important point is that you must have read the articles you are citing to ensure that you are quoting the author(s) correctly. Even if you have a research assistant working for you, you need to read what they have found. It is also a good idea, in cases where you are referring to a quote that the author has quoted from another article, to go back to the original article to make sure the information is correct. You will be surprised at how often you are misquoted in the course of your career! That is because the author did not take the time to read and understand what you wrote.

One last thing, some scholars argue that because their research employs the "grounded theory method" that they do not have to carry out a literature review. In this book, we do not hold to that view. As Fernandez (2019) writes, quoting Belk (2001), "An open mind is not an empty mind." We always need to know what has been written by our predecessors so that, once again, we can be sure that our brilliant research idea hasn't already found takers and that we are moving our collective understanding of the topic forward.

2. *Systematic literature review*

A systematic literature review is a structured, methodical approach to reviewing and synthesizing research on a specific topic or research question. It aims to collect all relevant studies, evaluate their quality, and summarize the findings in a transparent and reproducible way. The systematic review locates, selects, and evaluates relevant literature to address the research question. It adheres to a predefined protocol, with criteria established in advance of conducting the review. A protocol is a detailed plan that outlines the objectives, criteria for including and or excluding studies, search strategy, and methods for data analysis. This ensures consistency and minimizes bias.

An example of a protocol or plan is illustrated in Table 4.1. The plan entails formulating a research question, identifying research limitations based on the scope of the study. The scope of your research may be determined us-

Table 4.1 Study scope

Criteria	Scope
Population	Historical development of the music industry 1581 to 2023
Intervention	Development of music marketing research, limited by inclusion and exclusion criteria
Comparison	Comparison of factors related to music industry from an international perspective
Outcomes	Analysis of the music industry from a historical perspective over time

ing the Population, Intervention, Comparison, Outcome (PICO) approach (Wohlin et al., 2012). Taking the example of the music industry (Simonnot-Lanciaux et al., 2025):

Multiple databases (e.g., Scopus, Web of Science) are searched using systematic strategies to find all relevant studies – published and sometimes unpublished, sometimes called "gray literature." Here are two sample definitions for a *systematic literature* review, also called an integrative literature review. As you can see, both definitions refer to a specific phenomenon or empirical question.

> A systematic review typically focuses on a very specific empirical question, often posed in a cause-and-effect form, such as "To what extent does A contribute to B?" The term systematic means that the authors have defined the research question as clearly and specifically as possible and have made a concerted effort to ensure that they have found all evidence relevant to that question.
>
> (Page 139) (Kennedy, 2007)

It is based on the synthesis of one or more themes from the work done on these themes by a greater or lesser number of researchers. It shows the variety and trajectories of a body of knowledge.[1]

> The integrative literature review is a particularly broad form of studying the field of existing literature because it can encompass a broad array of scholarly literature – empirical, non-empirical, conceptual, theoretical – to address a particular phenomenon.
>
> (Page 272) (Callahan, 2014)

In a systematic review, titles and abstracts are screened, followed by full-text reviews, based on predefined inclusion and exclusion criteria. Each included study is assessed for methodological quality and risk of bias using standardized tools. Key data from selected studies are systematically collected and organized. Findings are synthesized – either narratively (qualitative synthesis) or through statistical methods – such as meta-analysis (quantitative synthesis) if data allow it. Findings are reported transparently, usually following the PRISMA (Preferred Reporting Items for Systematic

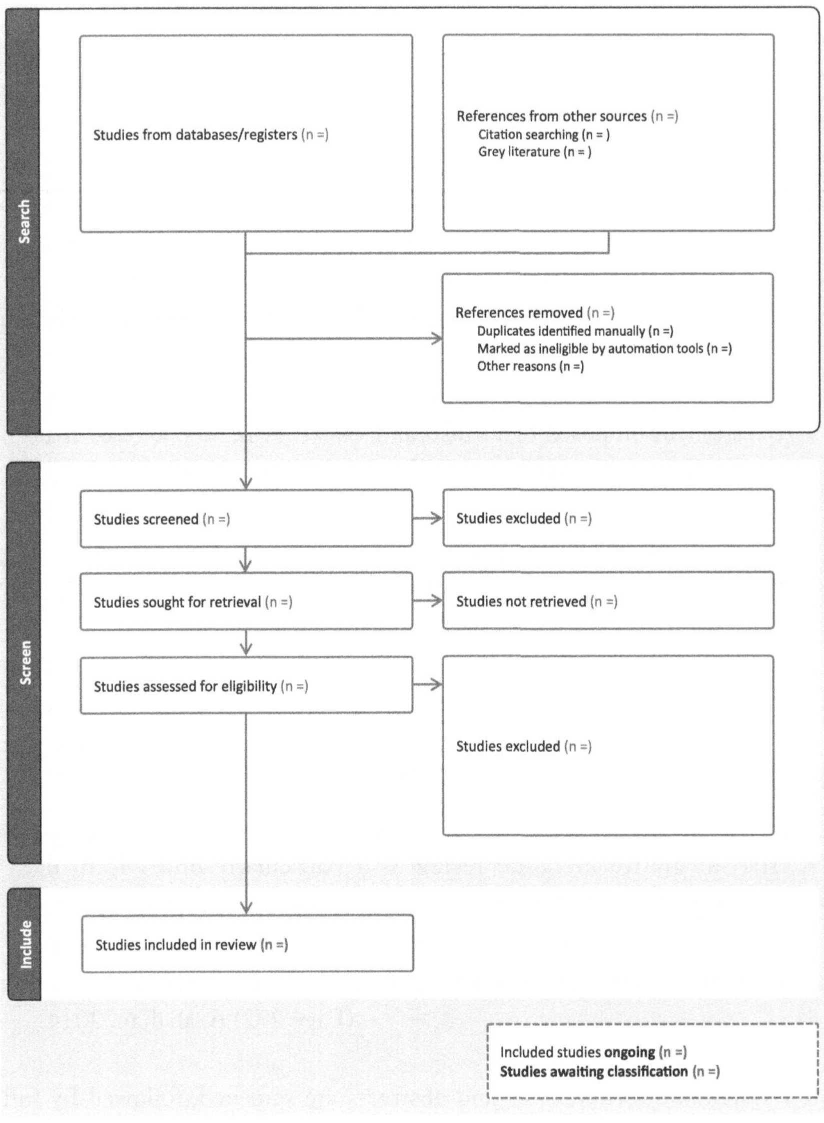

Figure 4.3 Example of the PRISMA framework

Table 4.2 Inclusion and exclusion criteria

Inclusion	Exclusion
Journal articles	Publications other than journal articles
Articles published in English	Articles published in other languages.
Articles pertinent to the study	Articles not pertinent to the study
Articles in selected databases	Books, conference papers, and reports

Reviews and Meta-Analyses) framework. The PRISMA framework is a process illustrated in Figure 4.3. The PRISMA framework provides guidance for selecting the articles to include or exclude from the study. You do that by searching key terms of key words in the literature and through search databases.

Inclusion and exclusion criteria can be tailored for your particular literature review. Table 4.2 provides an example of such a table, with suggested criteria for inclusion and exclusion, depending on your study's focus.

A systematic review is useful for the research community because it not only provides a structured overview of the literature but also allows researchers to point towards interesting avenues of research by outlining promising topics.

3. *Annotated bibliographic analysis*

The objective of an annotated bibliographic analysis is a form of literature review where you review a plethora of studies in order to analyze the current research stream and to assess emerging trends. In other words, one explores the intellectual structure of the object of research. Thus, one may want to do an analysis of cited references to uncover the structure and intellectual base of studies in a field. For example, Ashraf Fauzi (2023) did three bibliometric analyses in tourism (citation, co-citation, and co-occurrence of keywords); this research allowed them to describe the structure of knowledge in relation to the past but also to the present and to obtain an indication of future trends. It allowed them to find the most influential articles to date but also to determine the structure of co-citations. By identifying the journals, authors, and articles and deriving the major themes, a paper can make an important contribution to a literature subject.[2]

If you're pursuing a career as a university academic, you'll need to contribute to the growth of the body of knowledge in your chosen field and publish accordingly. One way of doing so is to devise an annotated bibliography of a particular topic. Make a point of reading and succinctly summarizing the articles that interest you. Don't wait for the moment when you decide to research a subject to start reading. Building up an interesting bibliography will not only speed up your future work but may also provide you with new research topics. Since it is impossible to read and retain everything that is published, continuous reading, note-taking, and record-keeping is a crucial exercise for you. You will soon realize that your bibliography can become a monster, given the sheer volume of articles published every year. It is better to get organized early in your career and keep up to date, especially as each research project you undertake will require its own literature review.

The three main stages of what we call an annotated bibliographic analysis, as proposed by Fernandez (2019), are: Assemble, Arrange, Assess. The first stage (assemble) involves identifying the relevant works and then searching for them. Once you've found the articles you're looking for, it is highly likely that the references at the end of those articles will lead you to other works you will want to find. When you think you have found all the work that has been published on your topic, you move on to the second stage. This is not to say that you will not find other interesting items along the way. If this happens to you, you enrich your list with these new finds. This second stage (arrange) means you must make some sense from the pile of work in hands. You will want to categorize articles by themes or subtopics, and next, you need to summarize each theme and subtopic to identify the major elements. In the third stage (evaluating), you should evaluate the quality of each of the articles found and decide on the relevance of the themes and sub-themes of your bibliography and what is relevant or unavoidable. By doing so, you will also be able to identify ideas for future research.

Keyword search through databases

There are several ways to build up a good bibliography on a given subject. Probably the most widely used method is to proceed by keywords, based on a search in databases such as Google Scholar. Usually, these databases can be found in university libraries. When proceeding in this way, you must first define the keywords you are going to use. You need to be as precise as possible, but at the same time make sure you are exploring the right field of study. It's a delicate balance, as too broad a definition will lead to an astronomical number of references and too narrow a definition risks missing out on important works. For example, if you use the terms "culture," "art," and "marketing," you will end up with 100,000 entries, the majority outside your field of study because the system will search for everything published with the word "culture" in the title, abstract, or text of an article (d'Astous et al., 2024). You end up with works in philosophy or sociology that are very interesting but totally irrelevant to your subject. Hence the importance of using relevant keywords. There's no simple method for defining what's relevant or irrelevant. Quite often the funnel method is used, where you start out broad and then refine your keywords.

Direct search of a set of journals

Some researchers choose to search directly in the major journals of their discipline. The risk here is to miss out on highly relevant and even important work done by researchers in other disciplines. On the other hand, it is an exercise that a researcher must undertake, if only to keep abreast of developments in a theme within his or her discipline. So, if I am interested in the consumer experience, I will want to know what is being published in consumer behavior/consumer research journals. I will need to consult all the journals likely to publish an article on the subject as they come out. If you do this on an ongoing basis, you will end up with a comprehensive and impressive bibliography, hence the importance of being organized.

For a new researcher or student, starting with the journals you are familiar with, such as *Journal of Management*, and reviewing each issue from a milestone year onwards to find the relevant articles gives you an overview of the subject. However, you should not rely solely on the title of an article, as the title does not necessarily reflect what is actually in the article. For example, the term management or marketing, or the words "arts" or "culture", may not be in the title but appear in the abstract. Even then, it may not be in either of them but could be covered in the text. If so, it should appear in the methodology section of the article. A brief review of this section will provide the answer.

A management researcher generally knows the main journals in their field. In the field of management in the arts, researchers from other disciplines participate in our conversation. To identify these other journals, you can examine the references at the end of an article to learn where the author draws his sources from and discover new journals. For example, in the field of arts marketing, there are nearly a hundred journals which have published at least one article on the subject since 1980. Many sociologists and psychologists are interested in consumption phenomena in the cultural field. There are even specialized journals, such as *Psychology of Music* or *Poetics*.

Students interested in museum and heritage management should consult journals such as *International Journal of Tourism Research, Tourism Management, Tourism Management Perspectives,* or *Museum Management and Curatorship.* The first three regularly focus on the management or marketing of historic sites and museums from a tourism perspective, which could be very interesting pieces of research. The number of pertinent articles published in journals outside the main publications of our field can be substantive. By way of illustration, let us take the case of a search this author did that lists all articles on *consumer behaviour in the arts* published since 1980 (Colbert, 2023). This exercise was based solely on a review of scientific journals. The result shows a total of 579 articles, distributed as follows: 133 articles in arts marketing-specific journals (e.g., *International Journal of Arts Management*), 177 in mainstream journals (e.g., *Journal of Marketing*), 160 in tourism journals (e.g., *Tourism Management*) and 109 in sociology and psychology (e.g., *Psychology of Music, Sociology*). Some of those journals have a very high citation index; for example: *Journal Personality and Social Psychology*, (10.504) or *Tourism Management* (12.879).

In conclusion, the best way to be comprehensive is to use both search engines and systematic reviews based on the journals themselves. It should be noted, however, that whether you use one method or the other, or even both simultaneously, there will always be articles you cannot identify, either because your keywords do not appear in the title, abstract, or text,[3] or because, in the second method, an article may be published in a journal you do not know. In our article by d'Astous et al. (2024), we proceeded with a keyword search supplemented by my own bibliography of more than 1,600 titles. The first method appeared not to list 600 articles from my bibliography, and with the second method there were as many missing. As such, no method is perfect. On the other hand, such a systematic review is more relevant when we want to publish a comprehensive review of the literature on a subject, as we then need to make sure we are exhaustive. For the literature review part of an article, the important thing is to be able to define the boundaries and the gap, not to be so exhaustive. We want to cite the most relevant work.[4]

4. Netnography

Netnography or *netnographic method* is a qualitative research method. The term is a compression of the English words "Network" and "Ethnography." The netnographic method consists in observing the communicative acts of members of a virtual community, seeking to give them meaning. For example, we can record likes, reposts, influencers, and keyword occurrences on the web, and then analyze and give them meaning. By using data collected on the web, the researcher can analyze consumer behavior and identify trends and other information. Chapter 9 gives a lengthy discussion of this method.

5. Meta-analysis

Whereas the systematic literature review is a qualitative compilation of published articles, the meta-analysis uses a quantitative method. It is used to determine what we know about a subject, but also to determine what we don't know (Kirca, Jayachandran & Bearden, 2005). It is used to check the robustness of the results of a body of research, to arbitrate contradictory results, to identify design problems and, finally, to identify avenues for further research (Grewal, Puccinelli & Monroe, 2018). This method makes it possible to study large quantities of data, understand the magnitude of the effects that drivers and mediators have on results in a management sector, and examine moderators that may explain differing results in the literature. Here's an example of a meta-analysis that illustrates the point.

> Across the many studies of motion picture box office success, unresolved debates and untested assumptions about the contributing factors persist. Using accessibility – diagnosticity framework and a meta-analysis of 634 effect sizes from 150 studies, the current article seeks to clarify the relationships of star brand equity and product reviews (from consumers and critics) with box office success.
>
> (Carrillat, Legoux & Hadida, 2018, p. 1)

Before beginning a meta-analysis, researchers must specify their research question and clearly define the scope of the study. Some studies aim to examine the entirety of published articles; others may only require a sample of papers. In this second case, it is important to precisely define the criteria which will be used to choose the material to be studied. The chosen method must be specified in the research report. The validity of this research will be affected by the inclusiveness of the sample amassed, the quality of the sampling method adopted, and the criteria used to exclude irrelevant articles.

Once the articles have been found, researchers must code the different elements to be studied. To do this, they must define the coding method and ensure that the coding elements are understood in the same way by each of the coders. It is generally advisable to use several coders, but tests must be done to ensure that each understands the task to be accomplished in the same way. A good method is to choose a certain number of articles that each person codes, then compare the results, and then adjust the understanding to arrive at a common base.

Ideally, researchers should have the raw material of each of the articles. This is usually not possible. In practice, the team calculates the effects for each article in the sample and then compares the articles between them before synthesizing the results. A good meta-analysis is done systematically and is replicable by other researchers.[5]

6. Spectroscopy

In the context of academic research, spectroscopy makes it possible to identify the most cited works, books, and/or articles and to show the evolution not only of the subject but also to highlight the texts which have fundamentally contributed to structuring a sector.

Marx and coauthors (2014), p. 751) offer a definition of spectroscopy:

> The quantitative method named "Reference Publication Year Spectroscopy" (RPYS) (allows you to) determine the historical roots of research fields and quantify their impact on current research. RPYS is based on the analysis of the frequency with which references are cited in the publications of a specific research field in terms of the publication years of these cited references. The origins show up in the form of more or less pronounced peaks mostly caused by individual publications that are cited particularly frequently.

Simonnot-Lanciaux and coauthors (2025) used this method to visualize "the chronological impact of the field's key references and how they have shaped it" (p. 43). They collected 11,565 music marketing publications found in Web of Science (WoS) and Scopus. From these papers, they analyzed a total of 35,481 cited references. After a series of cleanup moves, they were left with a final corpus of 35,481 cited references from the years 1581 to 2023. To measure the degree of influence of an article, they decided to retain only those with five citations or more. To graphically illustrate their results, they imported the 6823 references cited five times or more into VOSviewer.

Their analysis shows four disciplines from which citations have been derived: sociology, psychology, "classical" marketing (which includes papers discussing theories and concepts typically associated with marketing), and the specific field of music marketing. The authors were able to define periods with different characteristics from 1957 (it is from this date that knowledge has particularly developed and expanded). These periods are: 1957–1998 formalization of the concept of music marketing; 1999–2007 works on music as a creative industry, the study of music consumption, and the effects of piracy; 2008–2023 works on new issues in music marketing, such as the advent of streaming.

Conclusion

The literature review is an important part of your article. While the introduction to the manuscript serves to hook the reader, the literature review shows what your playing field will be and what conversation you want to have with everyone who will read you, from the editor-in-chief to anonymous reviewers and the academic public.

Demonstrate familiarity with the important papers written by others before you so that your work can be placed in the appropriate conversation. Define your constructs and, if necessary, choose a definition and explain to the reader why you chose that definition over another. Finally, if only out of politeness to the journal, it is appropriate to cite at least one article published in the journal you are targeting.

Notes

1 Ayala, Cuenca-Amigo and Cuenca (2020), Geyskens et al. (2009), Gupta and Mohan Joshi (2023), Tan and Sin (2021), and Woo Lee and Hee Lee (2017).
2 Some examples of Bibliographic Literature Review: Brown, Park and Pitt (2020), Hollebeek et al. (2022), and Montoro-Pons et al. (2021).
3 Note that you can proceed with titles only, but you can add a search in abstracts or even in the full text, at the researcher's discretion.
4 For a discussion and tips on preparing to craft a manuscript, see Dorobantu et al. (2024).
5 The reader interested in reading some more example can look at: Steel, Beugelsdijk and Aguinis (2021), de Matos and Rossi (2008), Kirka et al. (2005), Saha et al. (2023), Tanford and Yung (2017), and Yang, Xue and Jones (2019), Saha et al. (2023).

References

Ashraf Fauzi, F. M. (2023), "A bibliometric review on knowledge management in tourism and hospitality: Past, present and future trends," *International Journal of Contemporary Hospitality Management*, 35(6), 2178–2201.

Ayala, I., Cuenca-Amigo, M., & Cuenca, J. (2020), "Examining the state of the art of audience development in museums and heritage organisations: A systematic literature review," *Museum Management and Curatorship*, 35(3), 306–327.

Belk, R. W. (2001), *Research colloquium on multi methods & multi perspectives in marketing & consumer research*. Melbourne: Monash University.

Brown, T., Park, A., & Pitt, L. (2020), "A 60-year bibliographic review of the *Journal of Advertising Research* perspectives on trends in authorship, influences, and research impact," *Journal of Advertising Research*, 353–360. https://doi.org/10.2501/JAR-2020-028.

Bürger, T., & Volkmann, C. (2020), "Mapping and thematic analysis of cultural entrepreneurship research," *International Journal of Entrepreneurship and Small Business*, 40(2), 192–229.

Callahan, J. L. (2014), "Writing literature reviews: A reprise and update," *Human Resource Development Review*, 13(3), 271–275.

Carrillat, F., Legoux, R., & Hadida, A. L. (2018), "Debates and assumptions about motion picture performance: A meta-analysis," *Journal of the Academy of Marketing Science*, 46, 273–299.

Casadei, P., Bloom, M., Camerani, R., Masucci, M., Siepel, J., & Ospina, J. V. (2023), "Mapping the state of the art of creative cluster research: A bibliometric and thematic analysis," *European Planning Studies*, 31(12), 2531–2551.

Colbert, F. (2023), "Evolution of the literature on experiential marketing after Holbrook and Hirschman's (1982) seminal article," *International Journal of Arts Management*, 26(1), 6–18.

D'Astous, A., Colbert, F., Lamoureux, P., & Kyle, D. (2024), "Marketing the arts: A quantitative literature review," in *Proceedings AIMAC Lisbon Conference 2024*.

De Matos, C. A., & Rossi, C. A. V. (2008), "Word-of-mouth communications in marketing: A meta-analytic review of the antecedents and moderators," *Journal of the Academy of Marketing Science*, 36(4), 578–596.

Dorobantu, S., Gruber, M., Ravasi, D., & Wellman, N. (2024), "The AMJ management research canvas: A tool for conducting and reporting empirical research," *Academy of Management Journal*, 67(5), 1163–1174.

Euzéby, F., Passebois-Ducros, J., & Machat, S. (2024), "Exploring the impact of book influencers on reading intentions in the scroll era," *International Journal of Arts Management*, 27(1), 17–39.

Fernandez, K. V. (2019), "Critically reviewing literature: A tutorial for new researchers," *Australasian Marketing Journal*, 27, 187–196.

Ferreira, F. A. (2018), "Mapping the field of arts-based management: Bibliographic coupling and co-citation analyses," *Journal of Business Research*, 85, 348–357.

Fogg, B. J., Soohoo, C., Danielson, D. R., Marable, L., Stanford, J., & Tauber, E. R. (2003), "How do users evaluate the credibility of web sites? A study with over 2,500 participants," in *Proceedings of the 2003 Conference on Designing for User Experiences*, 1–15, New York: Association for Computing Machinery. https://doi.org/10.1145/997078.997097.

Geyskens, I., Krishnan, R., Benedict, J., Steenkamp, E. M., & Cunha, P. V. (2009), "A review and evaluation of meta-analysis practices in management research," *Journal of Management*, 35(2), 393–419.

Grewal, D., Puccinelli, N., & Monroe, K. B. (2018), "Meta-analysis: Integrating accumulated knowledge," *Journal of the Academy of Marketing Science*, 46, 9–30.

Gupta, M., & Mohan Joshi, R. (2023), "Art infusion phenomenon: A systematic literature review," *Journal of Product & Brand Management*, 32(2), 235–256.

Hadida, A. L. (2009), "Motion picture performance: A review and research agenda," *International Journal of Management Reviews*, 11, 297–335.

Hart, C. (2018), *Do a literature review: Releasing the research imagination* (2nd ed.). Sage Publications.

Hollebeek, L. D., Ghosh Sharma, T., Pandey, R., Sanyal, P., & Clark, M. K. (2022), "Fifteen years of customer engagement research: A bibliometric and network analysis," *Journal of Product & Brand Management*, 31(2), 293–309.

Hu, X., & Yao, M. Z. (2022), "Judging a book by its cover: Investigating consumer responses towards social cue in social media influencer," *Journal of Media Business Studies*, 19(4), 225–239. https://doi.org/10.1080/16522354.2021.1960721.

Kennedy, M. M. (2007), "Defining a literature," *Educational Researcher*, 36(3), 139–147.

Kirca, A. H., Jayachandran, J., & Bearden, W. O. (2005), "Market orientation: A meta-analytic review and assessment of its antecedents and impact on performance," *Journal of Marketing*, 69, 24–41.

Ladik, D. M., & Stewart, D. W. (2008), "The contribution continuum," *Journal of the Academy of Marketing Science*, 36, 157–165.

Marx, W., Bornmann, L., Barth, A., & Leydesdorff, L. (2014), "Detecting the historical roots of research fields by reference publication year spectroscopy (RPYS)," *Journal of the Association for Information Science and Technology*, 65(4), 751–764.

Metzger, M. J., Flanagin, A. J., & Medders, R. B. (2010), "Social and heuristic approaches to credibility evaluation online," *Journal of Communication*, 60(3), 413–439. https://doi.org/10.1111/j.1460-2466.2010.01488.x.

Montoro-Pons, J. D., Caballer-Tarazona, M., & Cuadrado-García, M. (2021), "From pirates to subscribers: 20 years of music consumption research," *International Journal of Consumer Study*. https://doi.org/10.1111/ijcs.12660.

Noonan, D. (2002), *Contingent valuation studies in the arts and culture: An annotated bibliography*. Cultural Policy Center at the University of Chicago.

Paré, G., Wagner, G., & Prester, J. (3 April 2023), "How to develop and frame impactful review articles: Key recommendations," *Journal of Decision Systems*. https://doi.org/10.1080/12460125.2023.2197701.

Pickering, C., & Byrne, J. (2014), "The benefits of publishing systematic quantitative literature reviews for PhD candidates and other early career researchers," *Higher Education Research & Development*, 33(3), 534–548. https://doi.org/10.1080/07294360.2013.841651.

Rentschler, R., & Liu, J. (2024), "Methods and methodologies in arts and cultural management research: A review and research agenda," in Y. Jung, N. Vakaria, & M. Vecco (Eds.), *The Oxford handbook of arts and cultural management* (pp. 59–76). Oxford University Press.

Saha, S., Rakesh Ranjan, K., Pappu, R., & Akhlaghpour, S. (2023), "Corporate giving and its impact on consumer evaluations: A meta-analysis," *Journal of Business Research*, 158, 113656.

Simonnot-Lanciaux, A., Gohoungodji, P., Perron-Brault, A., & Dantas, D. C. (2025), "A spectroscopic exploration of the music marketing literature: Origins, historical roots and recent developments," *International Journal of Arts Management*, 27(3), 43–61.

Steel, P., Beugelsdijk, S., & Aguinis, H. (2021), "The anatomy of an award-winning meta-analysis: Recommendations for authors, reviewers, and readers of meta-analytic reviews," *Journal of International Business Studies*, 52, 23–44.

Summers, J. O. (2001), "Guidelines for conducting research and publishing in marketing: From conceptualization through the review process," *Academy of Marketing Science Journal*, 29(4), 405–415.

Tan Hui, L., & Sin, X. (2021), "Flow research in music contexts: A systematic literature review," *Musicae Scientiae*, 25(4), 399–428.

Tanford, S., & Jung, S. (2017), "Festival attributes and perceptions: A meta-analysis of relationships with satisfaction and loyalty," *Tourism Management*, 61, 209e220.

Torraco, R. J. (2005), "Writing integrative literature reviews: Guidelines and examples," *Human Resource Development Review*, 4(3), 356–367.

Whittemore, R., & Knafl, K. (2005), "The integrative review: Updated methodology," *Journal of Advanced Nursing*, 52(5), 546–553.

Woo, J. L., & Lee, S. H. (2017), "'Marketing from the art world': A critical review of American research in arts marketing'," *The Journal of Arts Management, Law, and Society*, 47(1), 17–33. https://doi.org/10.1080/10632921.2016.1274698.

Xiao, M., Wang, R., & Chan-Olmsted, S. (2018), "Factors affecting YouTube influencer marketing credibility: A heuristic-systematic model," *Journal of Media Business Studies*, 15(3), 188–213. https://doi.org/10.1080/16522354.2018.1501146.

Yang, Y., Xue, L., & Jones, E. T. (2019), "Tourism-enhancing effect of World Heritage Sites: Panacea or placebo? A meta-analysis," *Annals of Tourism Research*, 75, 29–41.

Books on qualitative research

Birks, M., & Mills, J. (2015), *Grounded theory: A practical guide*. London, UK: Sage.

Bryman, A. (Ed.). (2001), *Ethnography*. London, UK: Sage.

Cassell, C., Cunliffe, A., & Grandy, G. (2018), *The Sage handbook of qualitative business and management research methods: History and traditions*. The Sage Publications Ltd.

Creswell, J. W., & Poth, C. N. (2018), *Qualitative inquiry and research design*. SAGE Publications.

Denzin, N. K., & Lincoln, Y. S. (Eds.). (2018), *The Sage handbook of qualitative research* (5th ed.). Sage.

Ridley, D. (2012), *The literature review: A step-by-step guide for students*. Los Angeles: Sage.

Wohlin, C., Runeson, P., Höst, M., Ohlsson, M. C., Regnell, B., & Wesslén, A. (2012), "Systematic literature review," in *Experimentation in software engineering* (pp. 45–46). Springer Science & Business Media.

Yin, R. K. (2015), *Qualitative research from start to finish*. New York: Guilford publications.

5
SURVEY RESEARCH

Introduction

This chapter opens the discussion on the different ways you can answer your research question through empirical research. We begin with an empirical method that is widely known but often misunderstood: the survey. Surveys are an appropriate method for researchers whose goals are to describe, explain, or predict a phenomenon of interest. They rely on self-report data, meaning that the participants report their own perceptions or recollections of their thoughts, feelings, and behaviors through short-answer and closed-ended questions. As such, the most important aspect of survey research is measurement. In order to be able to draw conclusions about underlying relationships between theoretical constructs, it is essential that the researcher can trust that the measures of these theoretical constructs are valid. Surveys are also typically used when researchers are looking to generalize their findings beyond the specific sample of participants to a broader population. The second most important concern in survey research, therefore, is that the sample is representative of the population of interest. If the measures are acceptably valid and the sample is acceptably representative, then the researcher is able to draw generalizable conclusions based on their descriptive, explanatory, and predictive analyses of the data.

Step 1: Selecting and sampling participants

The first step in survey research is to identify the population whose perceptions or opinions you would like to capture. This is determined by your

DOI: 10.4324/9781003487951-5

research question. For example, if you want to examine what motivates consumers to transition from subscribers to becoming donors, you will need to survey a population of current donors to a focal organization who were previously subscribers, and perhaps a comparison population of subscribers to the same organization who have not become donors. If your research question is focused on what motivates arts donors to make repeat donations, then your population of interest should include donors who have made more than one donation to an organization and donors who have donated in the past, but their donation behavior has lapsed. Depending on the specifics of your question, you may want to target donors who only made a single donation, or those who made a series of donations before lapsing. Simply defining your population as "arts donors" or "arts subscribers" will not capture enough nuance to enable you to answer your research question effectively.

Next, you must identify the source through which you will access participants, which we refer to as the sampling frame. In arts research, this often involves identifying an organization that is willing to provide you with access to their audiences, attendees, employees, or another group of interest. Many survey studies in arts management are conducted with a single organization, which enables researchers to control for factors that differ across organizations, such as artistic offerings, marketing strategies, communication efforts, and geographic location. However, these factors play a role in the generalizability of the study findings. As a researcher, you need to think carefully about how you can interpret the findings of your survey beyond your sampling frame, and what the appropriate scope would be for any theoretical or managerial implications that derive from these findings.

Once you have identified your sampling frame, it is time to select a sampling method. Research textbooks often draw a distinction between random and non-random sampling, which refers to whether random selection was used to choose the participants included in the sample. If the selection was random, each potential participant in the sampling frame had an equal chance of being selected for the survey. While it is true that random sampling methods possess better statistical properties, circumstances often limit the researcher's ability to collect a true random sample. The goal, therefore, should be to come as close to a random sample as possible, given the constraints of the population, sampling frame, and situation, and more importantly, to ensure that the sample is as representative of the population

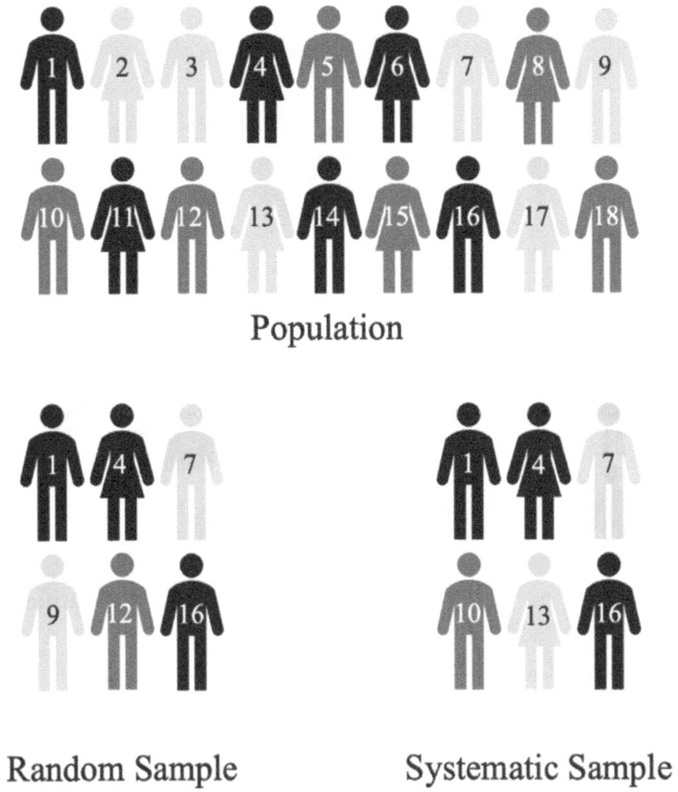

Figure 5.1 Examples of random sampling

as possible. Sample representativeness is one of the most important aspects of high-quality survey research and the key to enabling the generalization of findings beyond the survey participants.

Random sampling is possible when the researcher has a list of potential participants, for example, an email list from a partner organization. In some circumstances, the researcher may send the survey to the entire mailing list. In this case, the sampling frame and the sample are equivalent, thus the sample will be representative of the population as long as the sampling frame has been selected appropriately. The researcher may also select a random sample from the list using a random number generator or using a systematic method such as selecting every third person on the list, as in Figure 5.1. While these methods are random, this may not mean that the sample is representative of the sampling frame. Random selection might

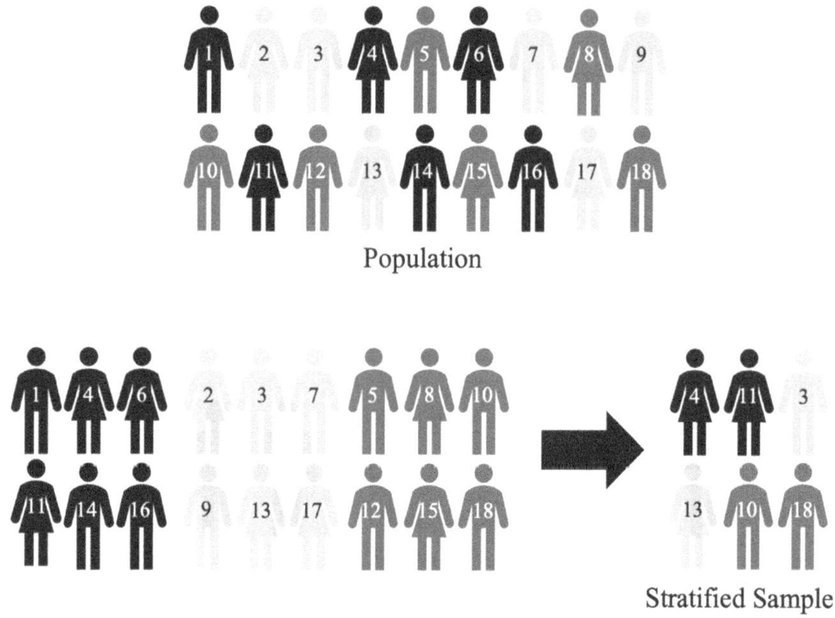

Figure 5.2 Example of stratified sampling

overrepresent female participants, for example, or participants who attend jazz concerts. The sample should therefore be compared to the sampling frame for representativeness before it is used for the survey.

If the research question involves comparing multiple groups of participants, as in the example comparing subscribers who donate to those who do not, then random sampling may not be sufficient. Instead, the researcher would want to ensure that the sample includes roughly the same number of participants who fall into each category. This is referred to as a quota sample in its non-random form, and a stratified sample in its random form. Essentially, the researcher creates groups or categories within the sampling frame (all donors, all subscribers, etc.) and samples an equal number of participants from within each of these categories, illustrated in Figure 5.2. For example, in Johnson, Peck and Schweidel (2014), we wanted to match audience members' perceptions of their relationship with an arts organization with the organization's classification of their audience members into single ticket buyers, members, and donors. We asked the organization to select 1,000 names from each group in their database to form our sampling frame

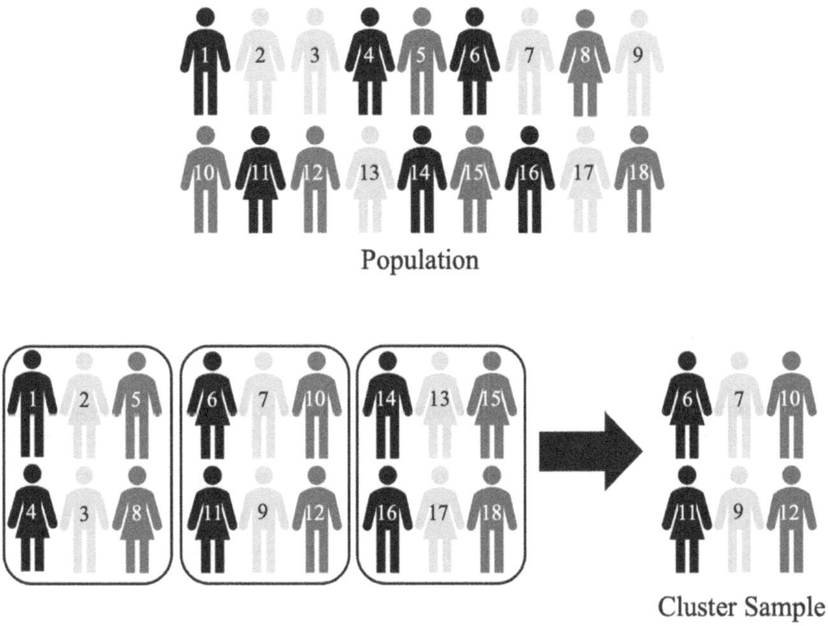

Figure 5.3 Example of cluster sampling

for the survey. If the selection within categories is random, the sample will have better statistical properties, but a good quota sample is still better than a simple random sample for this research question.

A final sampling method that deserves attention is cluster sampling. This is when a smaller, more specific sample is used to be representative of a larger sampling frame because the participants within that sample mirror the population of the sampling frame as a whole, illustrated in Figure 5.3. For example, researchers studying the success rates of new nonprofit ventures have argued that the state of Ohio is demographically and structurally similar to the population of the United States as a whole, and therefore patterns viewed within the state can generalize to expected results within the country (Mendoza-Abarca, Anokhin & Zamudio, 2015). Cluster sampling can be an efficient method, but it is essential to test the assumption that the sample is representative of the sampling frame, and therefore the population.

All these methods attempt to select a representative sample, but it is important to remember that the final sample will inevitably deviate from the selected sample because only some participants will complete the survey. Survey response rates vary, but will often be less than 25% of the original sample. This raises concerns about nonresponse bias, the likelihood that the survey recipients who chose not to respond might differ in important ways from those who did respond. While there is no way to test for nonresponse bias, some researchers estimate it by comparing the responses of participants who replied immediately to those who were among the last to reply. If these two groups do not differ significantly in their responses, this reduces the risk that the early participants were in some way unique or not representative of the population.

It is also important to remember that no matter what sampling method you choose, your data will be subject to sampling error. Sampling error does not mean that the researcher has made a mistake in their sampling method. Rather, it is the margin of error that exists in all research that uses sampling because the sample does not perfectly match the population. Even a randomly selected sample will not be truly representative of the population or sampling frame. As a result, there will inevitably be some difference between the statistics that are calculated from the sample and the true parameters in the population that the sample represents. Exercise 5.1 will help you better understand sampling error.

Exercise 5.1 Understanding Sampling Error

Try this exercise to better understand sampling error. Write the numbers 1, 2, and 3 on fifteen small pieces of paper, making sure that there are five 1s, five 2s, and five 3s. Since you know what is on the papers, you can calculate that the true mean of this set of numbers is 2.

$$[(1+1+1+1+1+2+2+2+2+2+3+3+3+3+3)/15 = 2]$$

Fold the papers and mix them so that you no longer know which is which. Randomly select three papers and calculate the mean of the numbers on them. Make a note of the answer. Repeat this random selection as many times as you like, each time noting the mean.

When you have enough data, graph a distribution of the "sample" means. You will find that it creates a pattern of variance around the true mean of 2, something like this:

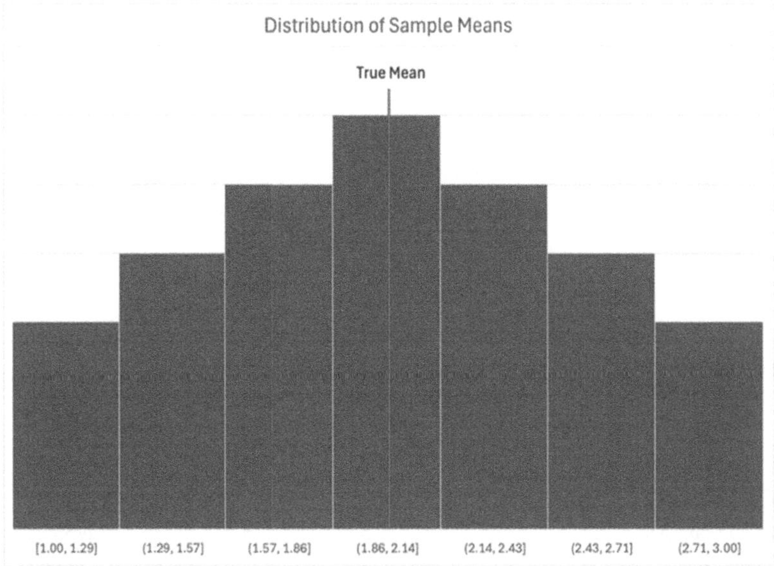

Exercise 5.1

This deviation of the sample means around the true mean is sampling error.

Step 2: Measuring the variables

Before you begin to build your survey questionnaire, each variable that will be included in your survey needs to be measured. The data you generate from a survey, and the implications that can be drawn from its analysis, is only as good as the survey measures.

It may be helpful to first classify each variable as either categorical or continuous. Categorical variables enable participants to classify themselves into groups, for example, single-ticket buyer vs. subscriber, first-time attendee vs. repeat attendee, or resident of City A vs. City B. Anything that could be measured as a multiple-choice question, even if the options are simply yes or no, is a categorical variable. When constructing a good categorical measure, it is important to ensure that the categories or options are mutually exclusive and exhaustive. In other words, each participant falls into one and only one group, and every participant can identify a group that they fall into. If the latter is a concern, you may wish to include an "other" option. If the former is a concern, you may wish to use a "check all that apply" question that permits participants to self-select into multiple categories. However, this is not recommended unless necessary, as it generates data in the form of "yes/no" options for each category, which is more challenging to analyze. Continuous variables enable participants to rate themselves at a point on a scale, for example, from 1 to 5, from 1 to 10, or even from 0 to infinity (in theory). While any kind of scaled or raw numerical response is a continuous variable, there are standard rating scales that are most useful to survey researchers. Several of the most common are illustrated in Textbox 5.1.

Textbox 5.1 Commonly used rating scales

Likert Scale

Strongly Disagree	Disagree	Somewhat Disagree	Neither Agree nor Disagree	Somewhat Agree	Agree	Strongly Agrcc
1	2	3	4	5	6	7

Bipolar Scale

Very Dissatisfied	1	2	3	4	5	Very Satisfied
Conservative	1	2	3	4	5	Liberal

Likelihood to Attend/Donate/Spread Word of Mouth/etc.

Likert Version

Very Unlikely	Unlikely	Somewhat Unlikely	Neither Likely nor Unlikely	Somewhat Likely	Likely	Very Likely
1	2	3	4	5	6	7

Bipolar Version

Very Unlikely	1	2	3	4	5	Very Likely

Willingness to Pay/Donate/Contribute/etc.

Are you willing to donate to *Organization*?	Yes	No	
(If yes) How much are you willing to donate?	________________		(raw number)

Constant Sum

If you had 100 points (or $100), how would you distribute it among the following?

Option 1	__________	
Option 2	__________	
Option 3	__________	
Total	__________	(Must equal 100)

How much would you say *organization* focuses on:

Contemporary Music	__________%	
Traditional Music	__________%	
Total	__________	(Must equal 100%)

While some continuous variables lend themselves to single-item measures, more complex theoretical constructs, such as personality traits, motivations, or perceptions, may require a scale. A scale is a multi-item measure in which each item captures a portion of the underlying construct, and the items collectively capture the full domain of the construct. For example, in Johnson and Grimm (2010), we surveyed audience members of a performing arts center to measure whether they perceived their relationship with the organization to be a communal or an exchange relationship. We measured these relationship perceptions with the two scales illustrated in Textbox 5.2:

Textbox 5.2 Example of multi-item scales (Johnson & Grimm, 2010)

Communal Relationship Perceptiowns:

I will give to this company to see them succeed. I will give to this company to support them.
I will feel good when I help this company.
I will pay attention to this company's needs.
I will give to this company if they need my help. I will help this company because I want to.
I care about this company's success.
This company's success will make me happy.

Exchange Relationship Perceptions:

When I give to this company, I will receive something comparable in return.
If I give to this company, they will give me something back.
If I give to this company, I will receive something from them promptly.
I will give more to this company if they give more to me.
I will keep track of what I give to this company and what I receive from them.

The items were presented in a matrix question with a Likert scale, where participants indicated how much they agreed or disagreed with each statement. Each participant's responses were then averaged across the items to create a composite score that represented the participant's overall perceptions of the relationship as communal and exchange. While scale responses are sometimes summed to create a composite score, averaging is more common and typically easier to interpret in further analyses.

Once you shift from a single-item measure to a scale, it is important to ensure that the scale is reliable. Reliability measures the degree to which all of the items in a scale are measuring the same underlying construct. It is based on the consistency of respondents' scores on the individual items. In other words, if the items are all measuring components of the same idea, then respondents should be scoring similarly on all of the items, within some degree of variation. Reliability is typically measured in statistics software through the calculation of coefficient alpha, which is reported on a scale of 0 to 1 with higher scores representing better reliability. What is consider a good alpha score depends on the complexity of the underlying construct. For example, the standard attitude measure includes three bipolar items, illustrated in Textbox 5.3:

Textbox 5.3 Standard attitude measure

Very Unfavorable	1	2	3	4	5	6	7	Very Favorable
Very Bad	1	2	3	4	5	6	7	Very Good
Very Negative	1	2	3	4	5	6	7	Very Positive

This measure typically has alpha scores over 0.95. However, more complex scales like the ones shown earlier would be more likely to have alpha scores between 0.75 and 0.90.

If your scale is multidimensional, meaning that the construct is so complex that it has multiple sub-dimensions within it, then you may also need to test that the data conforms to the scale's structure. In other words, you want to see that respondents' scores on Dimension 1 Item 1 and more similar to their scores on Dimension 1 Item 2 than on Dimension 2 Item 1. This is done through factor analysis, which looks for similarities in the responses to a scale and consolidates them to factors representing sub-dimensions. Ideally, the factors produced from the data should mirror the sub-dimensions that exist within the theoretical construct. Factor analysis can also be used to confirm that scales capturing constructs that are different but similar, and therefore easily confused, are being viewed correctly. For example, in Johnson and Grimm (2010), we used factor analysis to test that the items measuring communal relationship perceptions and exchange relationship perceptions were viewed as two different scales by participants. For more information on factor analysis, see Chapter 4 in Grimm and Yarnold (1994).

Finally, all measures, whether they are categorical or continuous, single-item or scales, should be evaluated to ensure that they are valid. Validity is a measure of the degree to which the measure captures the underlying theoretical construct – in other words, that you are measuring what you intend to be measuring. This can be assessed in a variety of ways, but at the very least, every measure should be examined for content validity or "face validity." Essentially, if you ask someone who is knowledgeable about the topic what they think this scale or item is measuring, their answer should match the researcher's intention. Measures that are more complex, or that are newer and have not been as well-tested in the literature, should also be assessed for nomological validity. This means that composite responses on the measure are statistically related or unrelated to measures of other variables with which the underlying construct should theoretically be related or unrelated. This is a separate process from testing the proposed conceptual model for the study, which represents new theoretical relationships to be tested. To assess the validity of a measure, it is important to test its relationships with measures of constructs that we already know are related to the underlying theoretical construct. If the correlations, a measure of the degree to which two variables are related, follow the expected pattern, we can conclude that the measure is valid. For more detail on validity testing, see Peter (1981) and Messick (1995).

Step 3: Designing and distributing the survey questionnaire

Once you have the measures selected for each variable that you would like to include in the survey, you are ready to design and distribute your survey questionnaire. While surveys can be distributed via traditional mail, telephone, or in-person, most surveys are distributed online. This typically involves survey software such as Qualtrics or SurveyMonkey. These tools will allow you to build your survey questionnaire within their online system from a set of pre-designed question types, as well as providing options for survey flow features such as skip patterns, display options, randomization of items within matrix-style questions, and other elements that can improve the participant's experience. Once the questionnaire is designed, these platforms provide a variety of options for distribution, including uploading email addresses into their system, generating a URL, or creating a QR code. In-person surveys may be a useful alternative to online surveys if the goal is to capture a small number of more open-ended questions during the participant's experience, for example, while they are visiting a museum or in the lobby between acts at a play. However, the time limitations of this approach make it less common than an online survey.

While there are no rules about the order of questions on a questionnaire, some questions lend themselves to coming sooner versus later. Screener questions that determine whether a participant is qualified to complete your survey must naturally come first. Demographic questions traditionally come last and therefore will serve as an indication to your participants that the survey is ending. Many researchers recommend starting with simpler "warm-up" questions to make it easy for the participant to start the survey and saving more complex or more sensitive questions for later. Finally, there are significant concerns about the impact of measuring the independent variable before the dependent variable, as doing so means that it is impossible for the researcher to know whether the effect of the independent variable on the dependent variable is due to their theoretical relationship or the measurement itself. Combining these norms and best practices has led to a standard order for survey questionnaires, illustrated in Textbox 5.4:

Textbox 5.4 Standard order for survey questionnaires

1. Screener questions that qualify participants for the survey
2. Warm-up questions that capture basic descriptive information, such as, "How long have you been attending X?" or "How often do you attend X?"
3. Dependent variable
4. Mediator variables – in reverse order if it is a serial mediation
5. Independent variable
6. Moderator variables
7. Control variables
8. Demographic variables

Control variables are an important component of survey research. Unlike an experiment, in which conditions are held constant to isolate the effect of the independent variable (see Chapter 7), surveys are subject to influences from individual differences among participants and situational or environmental factors, which can suppress the effects you are looking for, create the illusion of effects that are not there, or generally create statistical noise. One way to combat this is to measure variables not in your conceptual model that you suspect might co-vary with your dependent variable and use them as control variables in your analysis. By statistically controlling for their effect on the dependent variable, you can reduce noise and better isolate the effect of interest.

Demographics and other sample descriptors serve two important purposes in survey research. The first is to test the representativeness of the final sample against the sampling frame and its underlying population. For example, you can compare the means and distributions of descriptive variables such as frequency of attendance, tenure with the organization, number of performances attended, etc. with what you expect for the overall population. Similarly, you want to see that the sample is representative demographically, not overrepresenting one gender, age group, income level, or location. The second purpose is to serve as potential control variables to reduce statistical noise in the analysis. Not all demographic and descriptor variables need to be included in every statistical model, but it is worth examining whether any of these variables are correlated with the dependent variable and considering their value as statistical controls.

It is important to design your demographic measures to be appropriate to the makeup of your population. For example, if your sampling frame comes from an organization that serves the LGBTQ+ community, having only two options for gender will be under-representative and potentially insulting to participants. If your sampling frame includes primarily senior citizens or college students, a categorical age measure age with broad ranges will lead the majority of your respondents to select a single category. Some demographic measures should only be included when they are relevant to the research question. For example, measuring ethnicity or race might be relevant for research about diversity, equity, and inclusion efforts, but probably would not be appropriate for research about willingness to donate. Income or socio-economic status might be relevant to both of these situations, but not to research on the emotional value of an artistic experience.

Like everything else in your questionnaire, the inclusion and measurement of demographic variables should be considered carefully.

The self-report nature of survey research can also create common method bias. Essentially, because the independent variable and the dependent variable are being self-reported by the same participant, correlations in the data may be due not to the underlying constructs being theoretically related, but instead to the participant generally answering in a consistent manner. People are motivated to feel that they are consistent in their perceptions, attitudes, and behaviors, and this may bias their responses on a survey questionnaire to be unrealistically correlated. Podsakoff et al. (2003) recommend several solutions to correct for this bias, but the simplest is to capture the dependent variable from a different source, rather than from your survey. For example, in Johnson, Peck and Schweidel (2014), we matched the self-reported relationship perceptions of audience members to their behavioral data from the organization's database. For employee surveys, researchers sometimes capture performance evaluations from the employees' managers, rather than from the employees themselves. If it is possible to combine your survey data with other sources of data, rather than capturing everything through the survey, this may be a better approach.

Step 4: Analyzing and presenting the data

When you receive your completed surveys, the data will need to be cleaned and prepared for analysis. Incomplete responses may need to be removed from the dataset, missing values may need to be replaced or otherwise accounted for, and responses should be scanned for signs of inaccurate or inattentive responding. This is also the time to assess the reliability and structure of your scales and create composite variables. Some researchers will also recommend looking for outliers at this stage, responses that vary dramatically from the rest of the distribution, but it is generally preferable to analyze the full dataset unless there is a good reason to believe that the outlier responses are not representative of the population or signal inattentive responding. (For example, in Johnson and Cui (2013), we measured willingness to pay for a concert ticket and received responses of "a million dollars"!)

You will likely analyze your data using multiple regression, an analysis technique that tests whether a set of independent variables predict or explain variance on the dependent variable. Standard practice is to first run a model with only the control variables to determine which are correlated with the dependent variable and establish a baseline of the predictive power of the model, measured using the reported R^2 for the model. You can then compare this to additional models to see the change in predictive power when adding the variables that are theoretically expected to explain or predict the dependent variable. Your second model should include the same control variables along with all of your main effects, including all of your independent variables. If you have included one or more moderator variables that you expect to change the impact of your main independent variable on your dependent variable, you will then test a third model to capture the interaction effects. How you interpret these models depends on whether your research question focuses on explanation or prediction. With an explanatory approach, you likely hypothesized effects of specific independent variables on your dependent variable, which you can test by looking at the significance level of the Beta coefficients for those variables. With a predictive approach, less common in academic research, you are looking for the combination of independent variables that best predicts the dependent variable, and your concern is with maximizing variance explained.

If your conceptual model includes mediators, variables that explain the process through which your independent and dependent variables are related, you have several options to test their role in the model. Structural equation modeling simultaneously estimates a sequence of regressions to test the relationships between the independent, mediator, and dependent variables. The focus is on the overall fit of the model to the data, assessed through a series of goodness of fit statistics. This analysis technique can incorporate multiple serial or parallel mediators and multiple independent or dependent variables; however, moderation must be tested by splitting the sample based on values of the moderator and comparing the model fit across groups. PROCESS analysis, available as a macro that can be added to SPSS, tests mediation more directly by statistically decoupling the total effect of the independent variable on the dependent variable into an estimated direct effect and an estimated indirect effect through the mediator. PROCESS is able to test serial and parallel mediations and can directly test moderated mediation, including the estimation of an index of moderated mediation. Hierarchical linear modeling is appropriate when the data contains multiple levels, for example, if participants are from multiple organizations and the researcher would like to estimate effects at the individual and organizational level. The analysis estimates a regression equation for each cluster of responses and generates an average Beta coefficient across all clusters.

Survey results typically begin with a description of the sample and a table of descriptive statistics on the main variables in the model. A correlation matrix may also be presented to show the relationships between the variables. In a standard regression analysis, you would present a table of your models that shows the Beta coefficients and their significance level, as in the example presented in Table 5.1.

Results of a structural equation model are likely to be presented in graphical form, with the Beta coefficients for each relationship in the model reported and marked as statistically significant or nonsignificant, as in the example presented in Figure 5.4.

Table 5.1 Sample presentation of regression analysis results in a table (Alexiou, Wiggins & Preece, 2020)

Variable	Model A: controls		Model B: main effects		Model C: final model	
	β	*SE*	*β*	*SE*	*β*	*SE*
Campaign success × Age					−2,811.20**	943.80
Amount pledged × Age					0 29***	0.08
Campaign success			10,081.70	11,018.80	52,383.30*	20,798.30
Amount pledged			−0.11	0.93	−3.86**	1.32
Age			460.40	364.30	1,133.90	760.40
Full-time employees	9,746.50***	2,662.50	9,348.40***	2,740.50	9,661.4***	2,635.50
Board contributors	2,387.10*	969.6	2,277.40*	969.60	2,339.80*	942.90
Campaign backers	82.94	43.59	87.38	89.29	135.10	86.98
Theater	−9,851.40	10,946.30	−8,558.90	11,133.50	−7,763.60	10,724.20
Dance	−7,634.80	12,375.50	−6,317.60	12,474.20	−5,134.10	12,031.80
Jazz	−37,504.50	21,626.80	−33,186.70	22,063.80	−33,482.10	21,220.00
R^2	.26		.27		.33	
AR^2	0.22		0.22		0.28	

Note. Campaign year dummy controls (ns) included but not reported. OLS = ordinary least squares.
**p* <.05. ***p* <.01. ****p* <.001

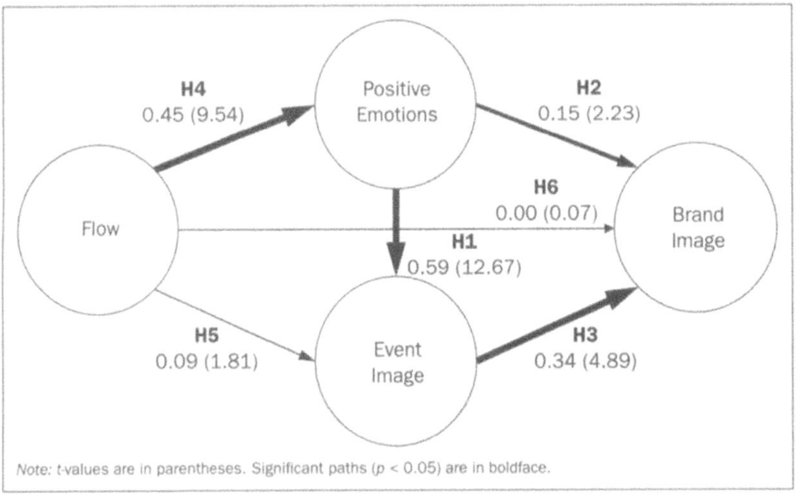

Figure 5.4 Sample presentation of structural equation modeling results in graphical form

Source: (Drengner, Gaus & Jahn, 2008)

Table 5.2 Sample presentation of structural equation modeling results in a table (Yi et al., 2022)

Path	Coefficient	t-value	P-value	Hypothesis
H1: Usage Barrier → Resistance	0.080	2.971	0.049	Supported
H2: Risk Barrier → Resistance	0.164	0.618	<0.001	Supported
H3: Image Barrier → Resistance	0.344	3.794	<0.001	Supported
H4: Self-Image Congruence → Resistance	−0.328	5.597	<0.001	Supported
H5: Resistance → Attendance Intention	−0.435	5.523	<0.001	Supported
Resistance R-squared = 0.189; Attendance Intention R-squared = 0.249				

SEM results can also be presented in a table, as in the example presented in Table 5.2.

PROCESS model results can also be presented graphically or in table form, with the direct and indirect effects reported as well as the Beta coefficients. They are also often simply reported within the text, as in the examples found in Massi et al. (2023) and Kottasz and Bennett (2020).

Finally, hierarchical linear model results are presented for each level in the analysis, as in the example presented in Table 5.3.

Most survey research will also report a list of the scales that were used along with their reliability statistics (alpha), either in a table within the text

Table 5.3 Sample presentation of hierarchical linear modeling results in a table

Variable	Hypothesis	Coefficient	Standard error	Relative effect size
Intercept		12.090***	*(0.105)*	
Main effects				
Movie level				
$SEQUEL_i$ (γ_{10})		0.273***	*(0.039)*	0.031
$BUDGET_i$ (γ_{20})		0.041**	*(0.019)*	0.015
$STAR_i$ (γ_{30})		0.060***	*(0.007)*	0.033
$REVIEWS_i$ (γ_{40})		0.055***	*(0.010)*	0.029
Country level				
IDV_j (γ_{01})		0.015***	*(0.005)*	0.023
UAI_j (γ_{02})		0.010***	*(0.003)*	0.024
PDI_j (γ_{03})		0.021***	*(0.005)*	0.027
IVR_j (γ_{04})		0.015***	*(0.005)*	0.023
$OPENNESS_j$ (γ_{05})		0.062**	*(0.029)*	0.018

Excerpt from a table from Akdeniz and Talay (2013)

or in an appendix. If a scale was tested for structure using factor analysis, the reliability and overall factor analysis results should be reported in the text. (Ex. "The measure had acceptable reliability (alpha = 0.XX) and loaded onto a single factor that explain X% of the variance.") Finally, if a scale was developed for the study, a table should be included that shows the factor loadings for the specific items in the scale.

Conclusion

Surveys are one of the most widely used and widely misunderstood methods in arts management research. A survey is a one-shot method, with no opportunity to go back to collect additional data or re-run aspects of the study. As such, it is important to invest the time and effort prior to running a survey to ensure that the data that is returned will produce high-quality results that enable you to answer your research question. It is also worth noting that since surveys are so widely and frequently conducted, there are secondary datasets available that are derived from surveys of either audience members or arts organizations, such as the US-based NEA's Survey of Public Participation in the Arts. Before collecting your own data, it may be worthwhile to investigate whether someone has already collected the survey data that will enable you to answer your research question. The advice for developing valid measures and designing questionnaires from this chapter will also apply to Chapter 7, where they will be combined with a manipulated independent variable for experimental research. Chapter 10 presents guidelines for interpreting your findings and communicating them to an audience.

References

Akdeniz, B. M., & Berk Talay, M. (2013), "Cultural variations in the use of marketing signals: A multilevel analysis of the motion picture industry," *Journal of the Academy of Marketing Science*, 41, 601–624.

Alexiou, K., Wiggins, J., & Preece, S. B. (2020), "Crowdfunding acts as a funding substitute and a legitimating signal for nonprofit performing arts organizations," *Nonprofit and Voluntary Sector Quarterly*, 49(4), 827–848.

Drengner, J., Gaus, H., & Jahn, S. (2008), "Does flow influence the brand image in event marketing?," *Journal of Advertising Research*, 48(1), 138–147.

Grimm, L. G., & Yarnold, P. R. (1994), *Reading and understanding multivariate statistics*. American Psychological Association.

Johnson Wiggins, J., & Grimm, P. E. (2010), "Communal and exchange relationship perceptions as separate constructs and their role in motivations to donate," *Journal of Consumer Psychology*, 20, 282–294.

Johnson Wiggins, J., Peck, J., & Schweidel, D. (2014), "Can purchase behavior predict relationship perceptions and willingness to donate?," *Psychology & Marketing*, 31(8), 647–659.

Johnson Wiggins, J., & Peng Cui, A. (2013), "To influence or not to influence: External reference price strategies in pay-what-you-want pricing," *Journal of Business Research*, 66, 275–281.

Kottasz, R., & Bennett, R. (2020), "Post-series depression: Mediating the relationship between screen fandom and abnormal consumption of screen-related products," *International Journal of Arts Management*, 23(1), 15–26.

Massi, M., Mion Dalle Carbonare, M., Prokupek, P., & Turrini, A. (2023), "Exploring fundraising executives' careers in arts and culture: The role of tenure and career switching," *Journal of Philanthropy & Marketing*, 28(4), 1–19.

Mendoza-Abarca, K. I., Anokhin, S., & Zamudio, C. (2015), "Uncovering the influence of social venture creation on commercial venture creation: A population ecology perspective," *Journal of Business Venturing*, 30(6), 793–807.

Messick, S. (1995), "Validity of psychological assessment: Validation of inferences from persons' responses and performances as scientific inquiry into score meaning," *American Psychologist*, 50(9), 741–749.

Peter, J. (1981), "Construct validity: A review of basic issues and marketing practices," *Journal of Marketing Research*, 18(May), 133–145.

Podsakoff, P. M., MacKenzie, S. B., Lee, J.-Y., & Podsakoff, N. P. (2003), "Common method biases in behavioral research: A critical review of the literature and recommended remedies," *Journal of Applied Psychology*, 88(5), 879–903.

Yi, J., Lee, Y., Suh, J., & Kim, S.-H. (2022), "Psychological determinants of non-attendees' resistance toward performing arts," *Journal of Business Research*, 149, 690–699.

6
DEPTH INTERVIEW RESEARCH

Introduction

The previous chapter was about survey research with fixed questions, statistically representative samples, and yes/no, multiple choice, or short open-end questions asked in a fixed order. By contrast, this chapter is about depth interviews (typically an hour or more), with small numbers of participants who may not be representative of a larger population, and a research protocol containing topics rather than questions and asked about in a more conversational non-sequential order with variable wording, probes, and follow-ups. While a survey provides "thin" information from a specific number of jointly representative "respondents," depth interviews provide "thick" more conversational information from a small number of "participants" and selective sampling is continued until theoretical saturation is reached. In other words, we trade off breadth for depth and representativeness for participants chosen for their potential knowledge and relevance. Furthermore, with depth interviews we seek rapport rather than anonymity as a way to gain participant openness. We may even conduct collaborative research in which participants help in understanding data and producing research output. If survey research is science, depth interviews are as much an art as science and depend on the skills of the researcher. Depth interviews are a qualitative research technique and may often be combined with observation and netnography, as Chapter 9 will consider. It may sometimes be written up in narrative form and/or produced as a video, as Chapter 10 will discuss.

DOI: 10.4324/9781003487951-6

Consider the case of opera music consumption. Specifically, we may want to know what the experience of consuming opera music is like in an opera house versus via live streaming versus in listening to as a recording. How might we go about using depth interviews, possibly in combination with other methods to answer this broad question? Perhaps we enter the research with an assumption that long-time opera enthusiasts may differ from new opera enthusiasts. We might begin with seeking some opera season ticket holders and an online group patronizing a site called "Opera for Beginners." Often, depth interview researchers are instructed to begin with a "Tell me about" question. We might begin with "Tell me about yourself." We might clarify that we mean "who are you and where do you come from?" This is as much to make the person comfortable talking with you as it is to elicit background information. We might follow up with "What sort of entertainments do you enjoy?" "What sorts of TV and movies do you like?" and "What sorts of music do you like?" Each of these questions can be followed with probes like "What have you watched/listened to most recently?" We might branch out to ask what others in their family including parents, partner, and children enjoy. We have probably begun by telling them (and getting informed consent – see the following – to interview them) about entertainment interests. After this "Grand Tour," we should have some general ideas about music preferences and we can begin to ask about music genres, use of streaming and livestreaming apps, concert tickets and subscriptions, what their friends like, how their musical tastes have changed over time, and other topics that may or may not have come up earlier in the interview. It is usually best to pick up on things mentioned earlier in the interview first and ask about others later. The depth interview process may be completed in one session, but if it goes long, it may be necessary to come back (for usually we come to them) another day. Or we may want to follow-up for further information as we get into analyzing the data. What follows is a step-by-step guide and discussion for conducting and analyzing a depth interview. We will also consider an entire project but will save a description of the write-up for Chapter 9.

Here are some examples of reports of depth interviews about opera:

Edelman, JA, Sloboda, J and O'Neill, S (2016) Opera and Emotion: The Cultural Value of Attendance for the Highly Engaged. *Participations: Journal of Audience and Reception Studies*, 13 (1), pp. 24–50.

Currie, G. and Hobart, C. (1994), "Can Opera Be Brought to the Masses? A Case Study of *Carmen* the Opera," *Marketing Intelligence & Planning*, 12 (2), pp. 13–18.

Claudio E. (2009), "Becoming a Fan: On the Seductions of Opera," *Qualitative Sociology*, 32, pp. 131–151.

You may want to look at one of these studies for comparison to the methods discussed in this text.

Step 1: Literature review and research question

Some people suggest avoiding prior literature in order to go into the field for depth interviewing with an open mind. However, we believe that an open mind does not mean an empty head. That is, it is best to do an initial review of potentially relevant literature for several reasons. One is to avoid duplicating what has already been done. Another is to find gaps that you may want to address in your study. And a third reason is to identify findings that for various reasons may or may not apply to your context and may necessitate further study. For example, a study of Italian lovers of Italian opera might not apply in your area or the methods may not be appropriate to your research question (e.g., listening to opera on the radio versus attending in person). A literature review should provide at least some tentative insights and should be critical and integrative. These insights should help you frame a research question such as, "How is going to Opera similar to and different from going to a movie?"

Don't expect prior studies to necessarily agree with one another. Researchers with more opera knowledge can probably get better data than researchers who know nothing about opera (or whatever phenomenon you wish to study). Some researchers are better than others at designing, conducting, and reporting a study. However, sometimes naïve researchers have an advantage in that they can ask uninformed questions and require participants to explain more carefully things that they themselves take for granted. These are the things that participants and researchers who are more knowledgeable keep silent about since they see them as unspoken truths. We also believe that "you can't step into the same stream twice." Just as a river continues to change, so does the musical journey of an operagoer and the operas they see and hear performed. Thus, the notion of replication does not apply. Future studies may reach different conclusions, but it is never clear how much of this is due to changes in the phenomenon (e.g., new operas or new interpretations) and how much is due to new researchers and different research methods.

With a tentative research question in mind, it is time to seek institutional approval. Institutions vary, and some are less familiar with depth interviews than others. For example, some IRBs (institutional review boards or the like) are more used to survey research and will ask for a list of questions. Given the adaptability of research questions, this cannot be done with depth interviews. Usually, some explanation and sample questions will suffice. In any case, they will want to see your informed consent forms. Especially if the interview is video recorded, it is good practice to use two-wave informed consent procedure. In the first pre-interview phase you simply seek permission to conduct and record the interview. If this is not given, you must obtain ethical clearance. Assuming that permission is given to conduct and record the interview, in the second phase, the participant is asked which uses they are willing to allow. This is part of ethical clearance, covered in Rentschler's Chapter 3 in this book. For example:

- Researchers only
- Students in a class
- Faculty members in a presentation
- Publication in a journal
- Presentation online or in a television broadcast

In the case of research conducted in Aboriginal communities in Australia, we also needed to get before and after consent from village elders to conduct the research and to present the findings we derived (Belk, Groves & Østergaard, 2000).

Generally, the participant is told that their identity will be disguised so they cannot be identified. But sometimes, as with a study of people with severe facial differences, participants were asked to allow their faces and first names to be shown (Cavusoglu, Belk & Kozinets, 2024). These permissions are most often paper and pencil but may be oral in the case of remote interviewing. Or they may be emailed back and forth in such cases.

Step 2: Locating participants and preparing for interviews

As we noted earlier, depth interviews don't attempt random or other types of samples; the numbers are too small, and the representative samples would be too diverse. But this doesn't mean the researcher merely uses convenience sampling. Participants should be relevant to the research questions and selected in a way that makes sense for the research topic. For example, for a recent project involving people with severe facial differences, Lena Cavusoglu and Russell Belk (2024) tried first to locate such people through NGOs (non-governmental organizations) offering services to facially different people. They refused to help, based on the fact that we were not facially different ourselves. After trying unsuccessfully using this approach, we went directly to facially different people with a presence on social media (Facebook, Instagram, Reddit). This was during COVID travel restrictions, so we began interviews remotely on Zoom and used snowballing to locate other participants globally. Eventually, we also secured help from NGOs in Turkey and India. Besides these countries, we also found participants in Brazil, the Netherlands, Australia, the UK, the US, and Canada.

This was a somewhat unusual ethnography in several respects. First, we secured the help of most participants not only in helping source other participants, but also in providing access to their social media blogs and videos, videotaping themselves fulfilling our requests to show various daily actions like getting ready in the morning and answering several questions like do they ever try to cover or hide their facial difference. And they sent us pictures from their childhood and offered suggestions for a video that we collaboratively made with them. That is, this was very much a collaborative video thanks to their help. Secondly, besides our written papers we also created a 16-minute video that we entered in the Association for Consumer Research Conference that was held that year (2023) in Seattle (https://vimeo.com/813448542, password: ACR2023LR). Two of our participants were so involved in the project that they came to the premiere of the resulting film and stayed for the Q&A that followed. When the film won first prize at the festival, they showed it and shots from the conference on their websites and social media, and others picked up on it and did the same. Some of the NGOs that had initially refused us then offered to help in the future. A third differentiating feature of our ethnography is that both our universities' human subjects' boards approved the unusual procedure of showing participants' faces and their real first names (which are normally disguised, along with blurred or pixelated faces). It would be hard to present a study of facial differences without showing faces. Using the two-step permissions procedure described here, all but two of our 19 participants gave permission to do this. Fourth and finally, we were not neutral researchers but engaged in advocacy research through PAR (Participatory Action Research) (see Ozanne & Saatcioglu, 2008). We continue to interact with many of our participants as well. It is hard to "leave the field" and we have become personally attached to many of our participants.

You may not be doing PAR, advocacy research, videography, or collaborative research, but the point is that participants today can be a big help in providing additional visual material. Anyone with a smartphone has a still and a video camera capable of broadcast quality images as well as sound recording. It can be an interactive tool through which participants can send images, video, and sound, including requests for post-interview additions, such as our request that our participants show themselves getting ready in the morning.

Step 3: Conducting the interview

Whether conducting the depth interview in person or remotely, the first consideration is to find a good place for the interview. In most cases this is in the participant's home. We have also interviewed people in their place of business, in restaurants and coffee shops, and in places of topical interest like theme parks, parades (with spectators), at fairs, in their vehicles, in trailer parks, and at special events like Mountain Man Rendezvous, where people reenact the 1825–1840 fur trade for a few days or weeks. The latter sort of venues also allow for participant or non-participant observation, as will be discussed in Chapter 9.

Sometimes it is possible to secure participants at the research site, but generally we try to arrange interviews ahead of time in order to allow them time to think about the topic, sign initial consent forms, and gather any special objects we would like them to show and describe, such as souvenirs from a trip, their collections, or their costumes, depending on the focus of the research. If the interview is to be conducted at the person's home or place of work, we would ask participants to help select a quiet place where they feel comfortable. If the interview is to be video recorded (see Belk et al., 2018; Belk & Kozinets, 2024; Belk, Fischer & Kozinets, 2013; Chatzidakis & Maclaren, 2018; Kozinets & Belk, 2024; Sunderland & Denny, 2007; Woermann, 2018), there are some additional considerations. To avoid "shakey cam" recordings, a stabilizing device like a tripod or gimble (Figure 6.1) is recommended. In-camera stabilizers are good, but a device of this sort is recommended. A gimble is especially valuable if you and the participant are moving during the interview. Ideally, the camera is held by someone other than the interviewer, and the same person can monitor sound with wireless headphones. In order to get better sound, wireless microphones like the set shown in Figure 6.2 are recommended. Even if you are just recording sound, such a setup can provide much better sound quality for easier transcribing. The second mike can go on the interviewer. Wired headphones and microphones can also be used but cables can be a hazard. In order not to backlight and silhouette the participant, try to have the major source of light behind the interviewer who is facing the participant. Editing can be done with free software like iMovie or the free version of Canva. More

Figure 6.1 Gimble steadying device

Figure 6.2 Remote microphone kit

sophisticated equipment editing setups abound, but these should suffice for most purposes.

For the interview itself or themselves, we have already covered the introductory grand tour. A depth interview is a special type of conversation. There is turn-taking, but the interviewer is in charge. Answers should be considerably longer than questions, or there is something wrong. In an especially long answer, rather than interrupt the flow of the conversation, take physical or mental notes. You should always be an active listener and not interrupt the answer unless it is going too far off-topic. Before trying to bring it back on track, try to hear the other person out. Allow them some leeway to complete their story or bring it back to the question asked. Concentrate on the answer rather than your next question, but try to transition naturally between topics when the chance arises. If someone has been talking positively about a time or topic, ask if there were any negatives or bad times. If they have been taking about the past, ask about the present and perhaps the future. If they have been talking about themselves, ask about their children, their parents. If they talk in generalities ask for specifics – the most recent occurrence, this week (see Textbox 6.1).

Use probes to encourage longer answers and pursue topics that come up that are of particular interest. If they are doing well, often a silent probe (or raised eyebrows or head nod) is sufficient to keep them going. You can add a word or two (ah, hmm, that's interesting). If that's not enough, ask more directly (Can you tell more about that? Or try a repeating probe, where you repeat what they just said but raise your voice at the end to ask a question and make an invitation to tell you more). If the topic is sensitive, give them time and show silent concern. If they can't reply after trying such probes, move on, but perhaps return to the topic later in the interview when they are more comfortable. Remind them that there are no right or wrong answers and that this is completely confidential. They are free not to respond or to leave the interview. Remember to circle back to topics that came up but that you made a note to return to later.

If the person seems reluctant to open up to you, there are several things you can try. One is to turn the questions about what they do or think and instead ask what their neighbors or friends do or think. This is a direct projective task, but there are more indirect projective tasks like the following:

- Cartoon tests (pretest the question asks and have participant tell you what happens next)
- Picture tests that ask for a story (e.g., Figure 6.3)
- Match the person with the brand (have illustrations differ in gender, age, class, etc.)
- Match the coffee mug or teacup with the corporation (show visual examples)
- If this brand/place were an animal/person it would be (e.g., Figure 6.4)
- Collage construction (find images online that represent an experience or concept and bring them into a Word or PowerPoint docu-

Figure 6.3 Pictures that ask for a story

Figure 6.4 If Trump was a dog he would be?

ment; then interview them about why they chose these images) (e.g., Figure 6.5)
- Sentence completion, word/brand association, word clouds. (e.g., Figure 6.6)

In general, projective tasks provide ambiguous stimuli for people to respond to. The methods can also be fun or play-like and offer an enjoyable task to break up the Q&A. They are indirect and get around socially desirable answers. They can be used with pre-literate children and non-literate adults. And just like memory, they are metaphorical and largely visual. An added advantage of using visuals is that rather than looking directly into each other's eyes, you are both looking at the visual (on a screen or hard copy you brought along), which this is much more comfortable. Another example: Retired professor John Sherry of Notre Dame University in the US had a class of students study a new brand of dog food. He had students take samples and interview dog owners. When they returned with their transcribed interviews (see Step 3), he said, "That's fine, but what did the dogs say?"

Figure 6.5 Collages: Female vs. male fantasy honeymoons

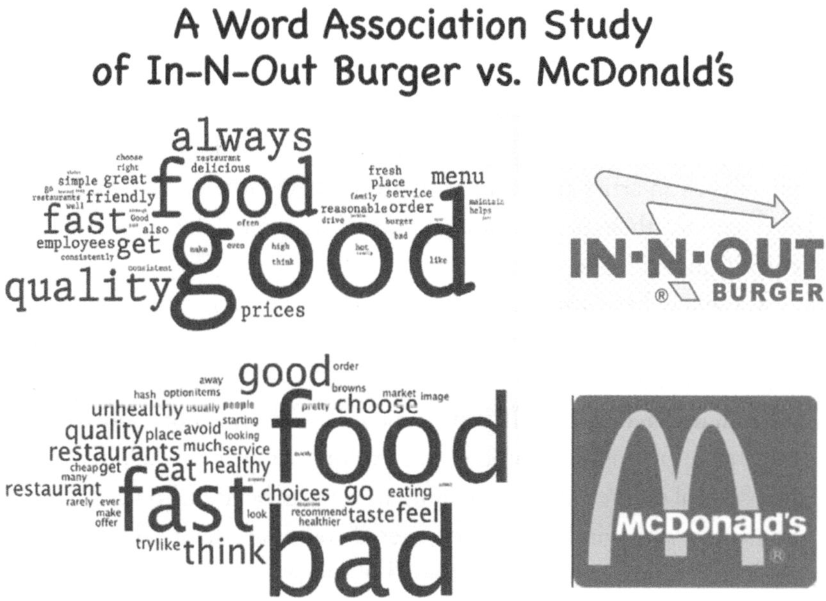

Figure 6.6 Word association word clouds

The students were bewildered, but they went back to the same people to interview their dogs. They opened the dog food and set it before the dogs as their owners looked on. They then held their recorders down near the dog and asked, "So how do you like this dog food?" Almost inevitably, the dog owners ventriloquized something like, "I ruv my kibbles and bits!" One final example: Ad agency McCann-Erickson was doing research for Black Flagg Roach Motel. The product involved setting up chemically impregnated yellow plastic squares in the shape of a building. The roaches were initially attracted by the smell and went inside the "motel." Once inside, they were overwhelmed by the chemicals and died. But the product wasn't selling to targeted women, despite consumer endorsement in concept tests. So McCann researchers had them draw pictures and tell stories. It turned out that roaches represented all the men that had ever done them wrong, and what they really liked was to spray them and watch as they writhed in agony and died. Their invisible demise in the Roach Motel offered none of this vicarious pleasure. For more ideas, see Belk, Ger and Askegaard (2003), Coulter (2024), Gordon and Langmaid (1988), Rook (2006), and Zayer, Russell and Drenton (2024).

Textbox 6.1 The interview

Exercise

In groups of two (or three, if you would like to try video interviewing), spend five minutes interviewing a colleague about their artistic pursuits as an artist and as an art patron. Begin with a grand tour, and also explore their parents' art pursuits. Use their definition of what constitutes art. Then switch roles.

You likely have a smartphone with you, so you might try recording this interview. A third group member can be the camera and sound persons. If you have a remote microphone like the one shown in Figure 6.2, use that as well. If you happen to have an iPhone, download the free app FinalCutCamera and explore using it as well. You can find several online videos explaining how it can be used. You can monitor sound with wireless ear pods, even if you have attached the remote audio receiver to your phone's port. Try using a tripod and compare it to trying to hold the phone steady with or without a tripod or other stabilizing device. Switch roles so that all three in a video group act in all three positions: Interviewer, Interviewee, and Camera/Sound Person. Watch and critique your videos. If you would like to also produce and share a video with the class, include B-roll as well.

Step 4: Transcribe, code, analyze

One of the most tedious but informative tasks with depth interviews is verbatim transcription of the interviews (questions and responses). AI and transcription apps can make this job easier, but the transcripts still need to be proofed and corrected by the interviewer. This is the point where you might think about using qualitative analysis software like Atlas.ti or NVivo. Unlike quantitative analysis software, such qualitative apps don't do the analysis and render a final result. Rather, they help the researcher organize data consisting of transcripts, images, and artifacts and look for patterns and possible code structures. They provide concordances, links to audio and video recordings, and apparent relationships in the data. Some researchers do not like these programs because they feel they distance them from the data. The alternative is to go through the data by hand and apply codes to potentially overlapping segments of data that may be words, phrases, sentences, or stories.

In a grounded theory approach (see Charmaz, 2014), there are three phases of coding. The first is *Open Coding*, in which the researcher codes anything and everything that may be of systematic interest. They may already have in mind some theoretical codes that they think might apply to the data, but others may emerge in this or later-stage coding. The second stage of coding in a grounded theory is *axial coding*, in which codes are merged, collapsed, expanded, and added to refine the meaning making that is taking place. And the third stage is *selective coding*, in which the researcher looks specifically for theoretically meaningful codes that help explain the data at a more abstract level and may entail structures showing processes or subordinate and superordinate categories. In the stories from the panels shown in Figure 6.3, some of the codes had to do with violence toward women, some had to do with robot violence toward humans, and some had to do with more complex gender and machine or human behavior. These were the superordinate codes. Participants who had seen one of the panels and were asked to suggest a story that might go with it in a graphic novel. It was also pertinent that the storytellers were either men or women of different ages. Three coders were working on the analysis, and they were also either men or women of different ages. The coder differences added diversity and depth to the analysis and involved discussions at each stage.

A fourth stage of coding that is recommended by Belk and Sobh (2019) is *abductive reasoning*. This involves stepping back from the data, applying some techniques like metaphors, heuristics, and semiotic chains (see Swedberg, 2014; Tavory & Timmermans, 2014; Timmermans & Tavory, 2012). Timmermans and Tavory (2012) suggest some creative means of approaching data abductively: revisit, defamiliarize, alternative casing. You might have a look at this paper and try to apply these methods to your data analysis. One specific abductive technique is to look for puzzles, inconsistencies, and anomalies in the data and to imagine a theoretical perspective that helps complete the sentence "This would all make sense if only. . . ." For example, in abductively stepping back from the data involving human-robot interaction in the study with the visual stimuli shown in Figure 6.3, we concluded that storytellers were invoking the metaphor of human slavery, and they believed that the robots were justified in rebelling because they were being exploited by the humans. This theory helped in understanding a particular theme in the data that we could then explore in greater detail.

Your analysis also depends on your objectives. You may have conducted the research to answer a specific question. But even in this seemingly simple challenge, there is room for deeper analysis. It may well be that rather than the answer being "yes" or "no," it may be that "it depends" on certain other factors. Also, even though depth interviewing seeks to get greater depth and openness through rapport-building, participant statements should not necessarily be taken at face value. Consider this possibility as well in looking for inconsistencies in the data.

Step 5: Write up or edit your findings

The section heading is meant to acknowledge that your final output from your depth interviews may be a video, a film (Lee & Rentschler, 2025), as well as a journal article, conference presentation, or book. Often the depth interviews will be combined with observation, netnography, and participant observation, as discussed in Chapter 9. The process of writing your findings for an article or book is described in Chapter 10. What is not included in these chapters is some guidance on how to make a video or film.

There is a short video by Joonas Rokka (https://vimeo.com/233296347) that nicely describes the sorts of topics that lend themselves well to video. As he emphasizes, video may help to express what people cannot readily put into words and instead focuses on what people do. But as the facial difference video ((https://vimeo.com/813448542, password: ACR2023LR) shows, depth interviews can also be a key source for video or film. To avoid being a boring talking-heads video also requires adding additional material and "B-roll" footage that can show what the person being interviewed is talking about or something that adds depth and understanding beyond words. We chose to show people getting ready in the morning, playing with their children, and discussing pictures of their childhood. Scenes of daily life can also help to humanize participants. Multiple camera shots can also help break the talking heads by showing different angles. Even with a single camera shot, it is possible to zoom in during post-production or to pan across a still shot in order to make it more interesting. Video construction and editing is a topic of its own that has been addressed in multiple disciplines (e.g., Heath, Hindmrarsh & Luff, 2010; Heider, 1976; Kozinets & Belk, 2024; Pink, 2001).

While video can be preserved and archived for many years and can be made readily accessible online, it tends to be more ephemeral. It may be seen in a film festival like the one that has been a part of Association for Consumer Research conferences since 2001 or the dance film festivals that showed Lee and Rentschler's (2025) two short films about arts and disability during and after the pandemic. But it then falls out of sight, except for a few possible other conference showings around the time it was made. There are archives like the Vimeo site *Films by Consumer Researchers* (https://vimeo.com/groups/136972), but this seems to have fallen out of use in recent years. And if the researcher is an academic seeking promotion, promotion committees must often be educated to appreciate that videos and films are every bit as demanding as journal articles and book chapters, and that they are competitively reviewed and juried into film festivals. And in our online digital world, journals like the *Journal of Customer Behavior* will accept videos and make them accessible along with word-based articles.

Conclusion

It is fair to say that depth interview research has been the cornerstone of qualitative research. It can stand on its own and be reported as a written article and/or a video, as we have just seen. Since arts-based research is especially visual, it is often critical to be able to show still photos and moving images. This is possible through archives like the one at UCLA (https://guides.library.ucla.edu/c.php?g=1030229&p=7466886), which includes a film and television archive as well as streaming video sources. Think about this guide more as input than output, though. Monoskop also provides an online guide to arts-related video material (https://monoskop.org/Video_art). The *Journal for Artistic Research* (https://jar-online.net/en/issues/33) is another useful platform for video input. There will no doubt be more video and film output journals in the future.

Besides being a standalone chapter, this chapter on depth interviews can be combined with Chapter 9 for more complete ethnographies. And in terms of writing articles or books using these methods, Chapter 10 makes a nice capstone that brings it all together.

References

Belk, R., Caldwell, M., Devinney, T., Eckhardt, G., Henry, P., Kozinets, R., & Plakoyiannaki, E. (2018), "Envisioning consumers: How videography can contribute to marketing knowledge," *Journal of Marketing Management*, 34(5–6), 432–458.

Belk, R., Fischer, E., & Kozinets, R. (2013), *Qualitative consumer and marketing research*. Sage.

Belk, R., Ger, G., & Askegaard, S. (2003), "The fire of desire: A multi-sited inquiry into consumer passion," *Journal of Consumer Research*, 30(3), 326–351.

Belk, R., Groves, R., & Østergaard, P. (2000), "Aboriginal consumer culture," in *Research in consumer behavior* (Vol. 9, pp. 1–45). Greenwich, CT: JAI Press.

Belk, R., & Kozinets, R. (2024), "Videographic and visual consumer research: The state of the art," in F. Kawaf (Ed.), *Visual methods in marketing and consumer research* (pp. 35–55). London: Routledge.

Belk, R., & Sobh, R. (2019), "No assemblage required: On pursuing, original consumer culture theory," *Marketing Theory*, 19(4), 489–507.

Cavusoglu, L., & Belk, R. (2024), "How to make a collaborative videography using phygital affordances to study sensitive topics," *Qualitative Market Research*, 27(3), 413–432.

Cavusoglu, L., Belk, R., & Kozinets, R. (2024), "Transformative netnography: Combining representation, social media, and participatory action research," In *Hawaii International Conference on Information System Sciences*, 2298–2307.

Charmaz, K. (2014), *Constructing grounded theory*. London: Sage.

Chatzidakis, A., & Maclaren, P. (2018), "On critical collaborative videography," *Journal of Marketing Management*, 34(5–6), 509–517.

Coulter, R. (2024), "A metaphoric analysis using the Zaltman Metaphor Elicitation Technique: Consumption experience as escape," in R. Belk, & C. Otnes (Eds.), *Handbook of qualitative research methods in marketing* (2nd ed., pp. 249–273). Cheltenham, UK: Edward Elgar.

Gordon, W., & Langmaid, R. (1988), *Qualitative market research: A practitioner's and buyer's guide*. Aldershot, UK: Gower.

Heath, C., Hindmarsh, J., & Luff, P. (2010), *Video in qualitative research: Analyzing social interaction in everyday life*. Los Angeles, CA: Sage.

Heider, K. (1976), *Ethnographic film*. Austin, TX: University of Texas Press.

Kozinets, R., & Belk, R. (2024), "Smartphone society: The role of consumer video in an age of ubiquitous platforms and devices," in R. Belk, & C. Otnes (Eds.), *Handbook of qualitative research methods in marketing* (2nd ed., pp. 410–421). Cheltenham, UK: Edward Elgar.

Lee, B., & Rentschler, R. (2025), "Dancing against the odds documentary and counterpoise dance film." https://www.adelaidefilmfestival.org/program/2024/dancing-against-the-odds, https://www.youtube.com/watch?v=RWb8RLqPkjE and https://www.youtube.com/watch?v=w7bxW9xL38Y.

Ozanne, J., & Saatcioglu, B. (2008), "Participatory action research," *Journal of Consumer Research*, 35(3), 423–439.

Pink, S. (2001), *Visual ethnography*. London: Sage.

Rook, D. (2006), "Let's pretend: Projective methods reconsidered," in R. Belk (Ed.), *Handbook of qualitative research methods in marketing* (pp. 143–155). Cheltenham, UK: Edward Elgar.

Sunderland, P., & Denny, R. (2007), *Doing anthropology in consumer research*. Walnut Creek, CA: Left Coast Press.

Swedberg, R. (2014), *The art of social theory*. Princeton, NJ: Princeton University Press.

Tavory, I., & Timmermans, S. (2014), *Abductive analysis: Theorizing qualitative research*. Chicago: University of Chicago Press.

Timmermans, S., & Tavory, I. (2012), "Theory construction in qualitative research from grounded theory to abductive analysis," *Sociological Theory*, 30(3), 167–186.

Woermann, N. (2018), "Focusing ethnography: Theory and recommendations for effectively combining video and ethnographic research," *Journal of Marketing Management*, 34(5–6), 459–483.

Zayer, L., Russell, C., & Drenton, J. (2024), "Projective techniques and use of visual images in a digital world," in R. Belk, & C. Otnes (Eds.), *Handbook of qualitative research methods in marketing* (2nd ed., pp. 232–248). Cheltenham, UK: Edward Elgar.

7

Experimental research

Introduction

The previous two chapters outlined empirical methods used to explain or predict a phenomenon (Chapter 5) and to understand a phenomenon from the participants' perspective (Chapter 6). This chapter shifts the goal to testing a causal relationship between two variables, for example, determining the potential effects of making a change to the arts organization's strategy, or searching for the potential causes of a phenomenon observed within the arts industry. Experimental research is the only empirical methodology that can test causal relationships. This is due to the unique structure of experiments that enables them to meet the three requirements necessary to demonstrate causality:

1. Manipulation of the independent variable
2. Random assignment of participants to experimental conditions
3. Control of situational factors to rule out alternative explanations for the phenomenon

Experiments create conditions in which participants experience different variations of the independent variable, and test whether this leads to different scores on the dependent variable, while controlling for other factors that could also affect scores on the dependent variable. This experimental control

DOI: 10.4324/9781003487951-7

is achieved through the second and third requirements for testing causality. Random assignment of participants to experimental conditions ensures that any individual differences between participants that could affect their scores on the dependent variable are randomly distributed across the different levels of the independent variable. Situational factors that could affect the dependent variable must be controlled directly through the research design.

In essence, the researcher must 1) randomly expose participants to different levels of the independent variable and 2) keep everything else about the participants' experience the same.

Step 1: Selecting the type of experiment

The first decision that an experimental researcher must make is whether to conduct a laboratory experiment or a field experiment. This decision represents a fundamental trade-off between the amount of experimental control available to the researcher and the realism of the experimental setting, illustrated in Figure 7.1. As Shadish, Cook and Campbell (2002) explain, the more control the researcher has, the higher the experiment's internal validity, the validity of inferences drawn about the effects of the independent variable on the dependent variable. The more realistic the experimental setting, the higher the experiment's external validity, the validity of inferences about whether the causal relationship holds across different persons, settings, and variables. In other words, the causal test is more stringent in

Figure 7.1 The trade-off between laboratory and field experiments

a highly controlled setting, but the findings are more generalizable in a realistic setting.

A laboratory experiment situates participants in an artificial setting that allows the researcher to exert maximum control over situational factors that could lead to alternative explanations. As such, it provides the researcher with the maximum amount of internal validity, in other words, with the strongest possible assertion that observed differences in the dependent variable were caused by the manipulation of the independent variable. Traditionally, a laboratory experiment is conducted within a literal laboratory space, where the physical environment is controlled to be the same for all participants. In-person laboratory experiments can also feature more abstract manipulations of the independent variable that would be less appropriate in a more realistic setting. For example, in Wiggins (2018), I designed an experiment to test whether participants could perceive a charitable organization to be part of their ingroup or outgroup and how that would affect their willingness to donate to the organization. Student participants came into our research lab, which had been decorated with red tablecloths and signs on one side of the room and purple tablecloths and signs on the other side (see Figure 7.2). Participants were asked to choose which color they preferred, put on a colored bracelet matching their choice, and sit at a computer on the corresponding side of the lab. They were then randomly assigned to receive a donation request from a charity whose brand matched either the color they had chosen (ingroup condition) or the color they had not chosen (outgroup condition) and asked whether they would donate to the charity. This is clearly not a realistic situation in which a charitable donation request would be made, but it allowed for a tightly controlled test of the independent variable.

Laboratory experiments can also be conducted online using survey software such as Qualtrics or SurveyMonkey. The key is to ensure that the participants' experience of the online questionnaire is identical except for the manipulation of the independent variable. For example, in Johnson and Cui (2013), we designed an online scenario-based experiment in which participants were asked to imagine that a band or singer they wanted to see in concert was coming to their area and they were using a website to purchase tickets. Participants were all told that the concert was using a pay-what-you-want pricing strategy and were randomly assigned to receive one of four messages providing different reference prices: a minimum price, a maximum

Figure 7.2 Example of an in-person laboratory experiment
Source: (Wiggins, 2018)

price, a suggested price, or a control condition with no reference price. We then measured the price they intended to pay to see the impact of the reference price on willingness to pay. Every aspect of the online questionnaire except for the reference price message was kept identical in order to isolate the effect of the reference price and control for any alternative explanations.

Field experiments, in contrast, are conducted within a real setting in which participants would naturally encounter the phenomenon being tested. This increased realism provides greater confidence that the experimental results provide a valid representation of how people would respond to the phenomenon outside of a research setting, and therefore greater external validity and generalizability. Field experiments can be conducted within a physical space in which the phenomenon would really occur. For example, in Cui and Wiggins (2017), we partnered with a jazz club that featured performances where they "passed the hat" at the set break to collect cash tips for the performers, a natural pay-what-you-want setting. Across eight performances, we varied the message the club manager used to ask the audience to contribute to invite the audience to pay-what-you-want, pay-what-you-can, or pay-what-you-think-it's-worth. We measured the total amount contributed, the number of audience members who contributed, and the total number of audience members in attendance, which enabled us to calculate the percentage of audience members who paid and the average amount paid as our dependent variables.

Field experiments can also be conducted via mail or email if this is a realistic setting in which the phenomenon would occur. For example, in Peck and Johnson (2011), we tested the impact of touch on persuasion by partnering with a symphony orchestra that was hosting a New Year's Ball as a fundraising event. The symphony planned to send paper invitations by mail to 4,000 prospective attendees. We attached a band around the outside of the invitation that had to be removed in order to open the invitation, to ensure that participants would touch the band (see Figure 7.3). Half the 4,000 invitations featured a paper band; the other half featured a velvet band. We included a questionnaire with the invitation that measured participants' likelihood of attending the event along with other relevant measures, which was returned to us directly via a prepaid envelope. This allowed us to test whether having the velvet band, a positively valenced touch element, was more persuasive than the neutral paper band.

All of these examples except for the jazz club are considered true experiments in that they meet all three criteria for testing causality: manipulation of the independent variable, random assignment of participants to conditions, and control of situational factors that could affect the dependent variable. The jazz club experiment meets two of these criteria, manipulation and control, but participants at the jazz club were not ran-

Figure 7.3 Example of a field experiment conducted by mail
Source: (Peck & Johnson, 2011)

domly assigned to the different message conditions. Rather, the messages were randomly presented at different performances and participants self-selected into a condition by choosing which performance to attend. This is an example of a quasi-experiment, a study in which the independent variable is manipulated, and the situation is controlled, but there is no random assignment of participants to conditions. Quasi-experimental designs might feature an independent variable that is manipulated geographically – running one advertisement in City A and another in City B, for example – or at different times. For example, Loureiro, Roschk and Lima (2019) varied the music being played in an art gallery on different days to see the effect it had on visitors' experience, memories, and willingness to spread positive word of mouth about the gallery. Quasi-experiments are most often found in field experiments, since laboratory experiments enable the researcher to have maximum control over the setting and design, including random assignment.

One final design that deserves mention is a natural experiment. This is when the researcher does not manipulate the independent variable, but rather a change in the environment naturally creates experimental conditions that enable the researcher to examine the phenomenon before and after the change occurred. This type of experiment is common in economics, examining the impact of sudden changes in the economic environment such as a stock market crash, and in accounting, examining the impact of a new regulation or policy. In the early 2020s, a number of studies examined shifts in arts consumption and organizational strategies in response to the COVID-19 pandemic. These studies that examined the same phenomenon before, during, and after the pandemic would also be examples of natural experiments. Natural experiments typically rely on secondary data and use time series analysis or difference-in-difference analysis, but in some settings, they can involve the collection of primary data before and after the environmental change. When possible, natural experiments should include a control group for comparison purposes.

Determining the type of experiment naturally incorporates selecting the sample of participants. The sample selection process for experiments follows the same guidelines as for surveys, as discussed in Chapter 5.

Step 2: Determining the factorial design

Once you have selected the type of experiment, the next step is to specify the factorial design, which determines how many conditions will be in the experiment and how these conditions will differ from each other. The relevant questions at this stage are 1) how many independent variables, or factors, are included in the design, 2) how many of these independent variables are being manipulated, and 3) how many levels or conditions each manipulated variable includes.

The simplest factorial design is a one-factor, two-level design – one independent variable with two conditions. This can take the form of a treatment vs. control design in which the independent variable of interest is either present or absent. For example, Wang, Xu and Zhang (2022) conducted a field experiment at a metro station in Shanghai that featured an art exhibition from London's National Gallery to test whether exposure to art increased consumers' interest in luxury consumption. The researchers approached consumers who had viewed the art exhibition (treatment) and those who had not (control) and measured their interest in visiting a luxury shopping mall nearby. Similarly, in a laboratory experiment, Hoffmann and Coate (2022) showed participants pairs of artworks painted by one male and one female artist and either revealed the artists' gender (treatment) or did not (control) to examine gender discrimination in the art market. Another common version of a one-factor, two-level design is an A/B test in which two different versions of the independent variable are compared. For example, Joye and Fennis (2024) test the effect of cardinal (orthogonal) (A) vs. oblique (tilted) (B) artwork on music albums and find that consumers listen longer to music when the album artwork is cardinal than when it is oblique. An example of this artwork appears later in the chapter. A one-factor design can also be extended to more than two conditions, as in Cui and Wiggins (2017) when we compared three pay-what-you-want messages to determine which resulted in the highest revenue yield for the organization.

Condition 1	Condition 2
Treatment or Version A	Control or Version B

A variation on the one-factor design is a nested design, a treatment vs. control design in which multiple treatment conditions are nested within the treatment condition. This is essentially an A/B design with an added control condition. For example, Baumgarth and Wieker (2020) examined the artification of products and tested three different types of art – fine art, street art, and graffiti – against a non-art control condition. In their laboratory experiment, Loureiro, Roschk and Lima (2019) tested two different types of music against a control condition with no music. In Johnson and Cui (2013), we tested three different reference prices against a control condition with no reference price given. And in Wiggins et al. (2017), we tested three different strategic responses to negative critic reviews against a control condition in which the organization did not respond.

Condition 1 Treatment Version A	Condition 2 Treatment Version B	Condition 3 Treatment Version C	Condition 4 Control

Many experimental studies include a manipulated moderator variable as well as a manipulated independent variable. Assuming that each variable, or factor, only has two conditions, this becomes a 2 x 2 factorial design. For example, Hernando and Campo (2017) randomly assigned participants to view paintings by a mid-career artist and a young artist and either revealed or withheld each artist's name. This was a 2 (artist career stage: mid-career vs. young) x 2 (artist's name: present vs. absent) design that yielded four conditions:

Condition 1 Mid-Career Artist with Name Young Artist with Name	Condition 2 Mid-Career Artist without Name Young Artist with Name
Condition 3 Mid-Career Artist with Name Young Artist without Name	Condition 4 Mid-Career Artist without Name Young Artist without Name

As with the one-factor, two-level design, factorial designs can be extended to have more than two levels within each factor.

All of the designs presented thus far are considered between-subjects designs, meaning that different participants are assigned to the different conditions. It is also possible to conduct an experiment using a within-subjects design, also referred to as a repeated measures design. This is when responses to the dependent variable are collected from the same participant at two different points in time, often before and after an experimental treatment. Participants' responses at Time 2 are then compared to their own responses at Time 1, hence the term within-subjects. For example, Hale and Woronkowicz (2019) measured students' level of arts participation and perceived barriers to arts involvement before and after a university's investment in free arts programming, and used the changes in participants' responses to test the impact of the investment. While this variable was measured at each time period, this is still considered an experimental factor as time is the manipulated independent variable (before vs. after). It is also possible to test a mixed design in which one factor is measured within subjects at different points in time and the other factor is manipulated between subjects.

Step 3: Designing and pretesting the manipulations

Once you have selected an experiment type and determined the factorial design, the next step is to design the manipulations for your independent variable. This is the most creative component of experimental design.

Depending on the variable you are trying to manipulate, your manipulations may take the form of text, either a simple statement or a longer description of an organization or scenario, as illustrated in Figure 7.4.

Your manipulations may also be visual images, whether images of real artwork as in Hernando and Campo (2017) or Hoffmann and Coate (2022), fictional creations based on artwork (see Figure 7.5 and Figure 7.6), or original visual creations.

Your manipulations may also include videos, music, tangible elements, or even actions. For example, Broekman et al. (2019) used choreography to manipulate the type of solidarity displayed in a dance performance and

Imagine that you have decided to go to the concert. You call up the box office to order tickets. When you ask how much the tickets will cost, the box office operator replies:

"Our pricing policy lets you decide the amount you would like to pay for your tickets. All tickets are general admission, so the price you pay will not affect where you sit at the concert. All of our seats have excellent views, so you will have a great experience no matter where you sit. **You can choose a price to pay between $20.00 and $50.00 per ticket.** How much would you like to pay?"

4 How much will you pay for your ticket?

Figure 7.4 Example of a scenario-based manipulation
Source: (Johnson & Cui, 2013)

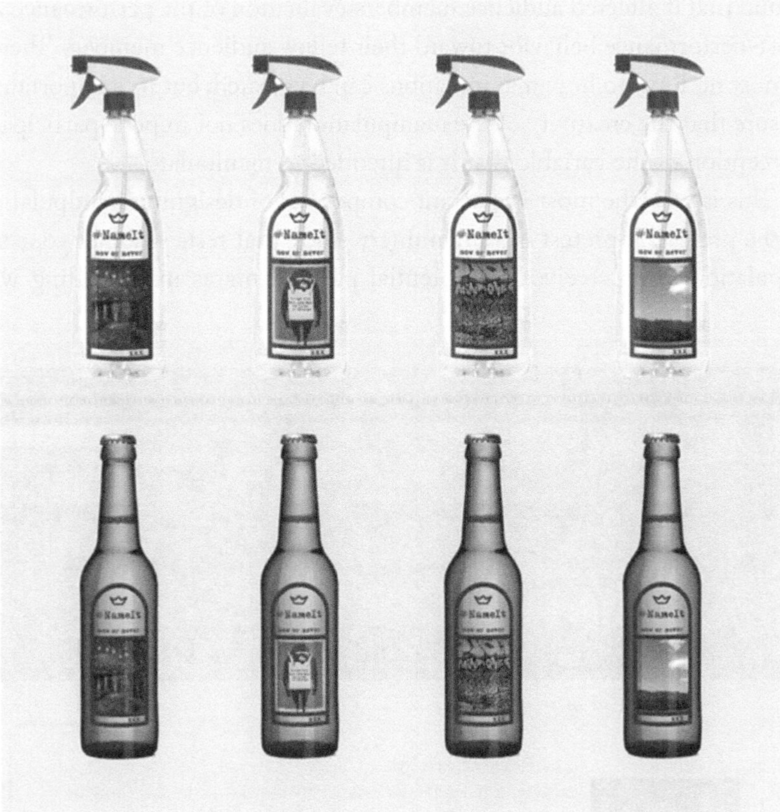

Figure 7.5 Example of fictional manipulations created from artwork
Source: (Baumgarth & Wieker, 2020)

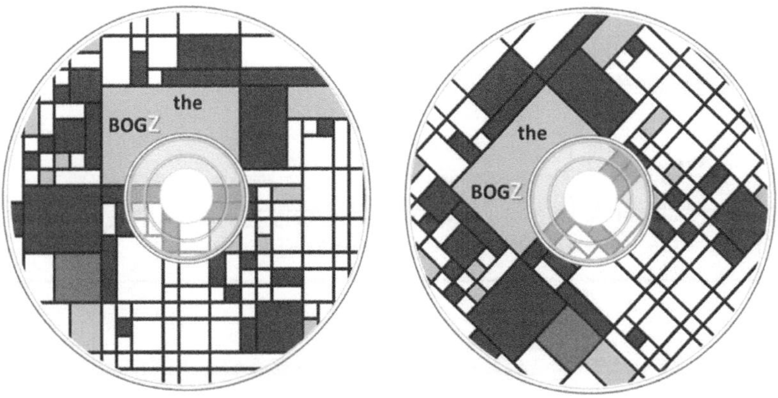

Figure 7.6 Example of fictional manipulations created from artwork
Source: (Joye & Fennis, 2024)

found that it affected audience members' evaluation of the performance and post-performance behavior toward their fellow audience members. There is almost no limit to how manipulations can be created, but it is important to ensure that the creativity of the manipulation does not impede participants' perception of the variable that it is intended to manipulate.

This is why the most important component of designing manipulations is the pretest. A pretest is a preliminary study that tests whether your manipulations are perceived by potential participants as manipulating what

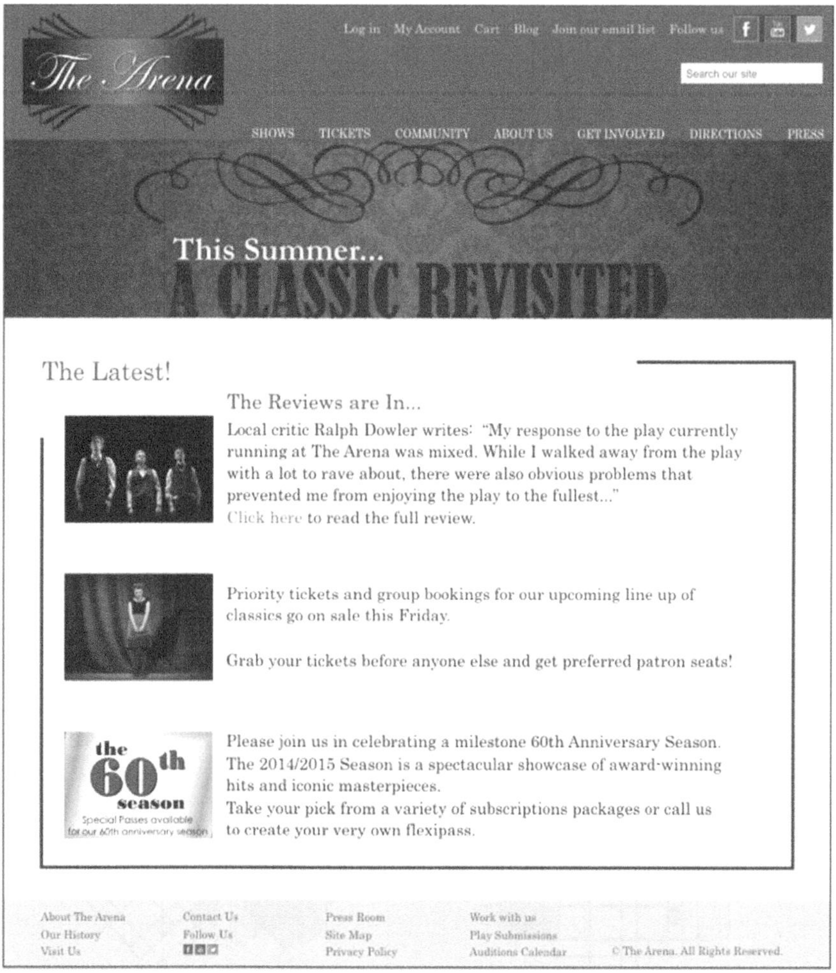

Figure 7.7 Example of a fictional website manipulation

Source: (Wiggins et al., 2017)

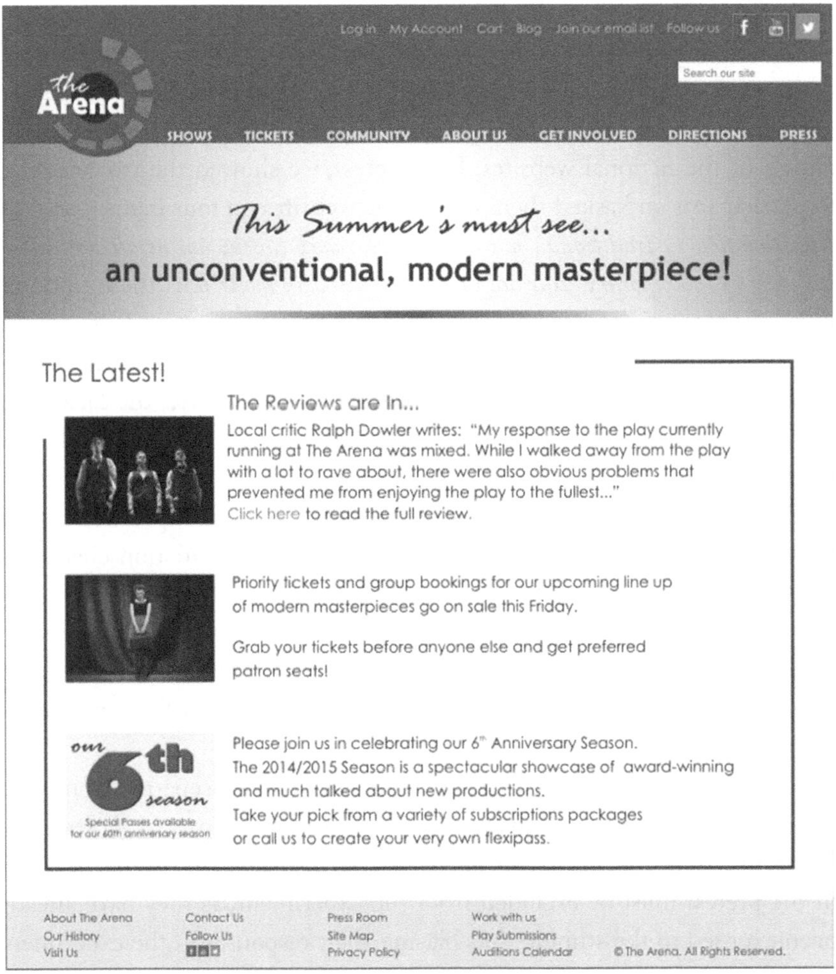

Figure 7.7 (Continued)

they are intended to. To conduct a pretest, you first choose a small sample of participants that are similar to or representative of the sample that will take part in the eventual experiment. You present the manipulations to these participants exactly as you will in the experiment. However, instead of measuring the dependent variable or other measures that you will use in your final experiment, you instead ask them to complete a measure of the *independent* variable that the manipulation is intended to manipulate. For example, in Wiggins et al. (2017), we used fictional websites to manipulate whether the arts organization was perceived as presenting traditional or contemporary theater (see Figure 7.7). We manipulated this variable of *genre* through the textual description of the play and theater as well as the design of the fictional websites. In a pretest, we showed the two websites to participants and asked them to rate the websites on four items: *not at all traditional/very traditional, not at all classic/very classic, not at all contemporary/very contemporary,* and *not at all modern/very modern.* If the traditional website scored significantly higher than the contemporary website on the first two items, and significantly lower on the second two items, we would conclude that the manipulation was effective. In this case, the latter was true, but the former was not, so the traditional website was updated before the final study.

Even if your manipulation passes the pretest, a manipulation check should also be included in your experiment. The manipulation check can use the same measure that is used in the pretest and should be tested before any analyses are conducted using the manipulated independent variable. This provides an additional check that participants in the experiment viewed the manipulations as representing different levels of the independent variable.

It is important that any pretests conducted remain separate from your main experiment. The data may not be combined as the pretest serves a different function from the experiment. In addition, anyone who participated in the pretest must be excluded from the experiment, as they have already been exposed to the stimuli, thus biasing their responses in the experiment and corrupting your design. For the same reason, if you run a series of experiments, anyone who participates in the first experiment must be excluded from any future experiments, and so on.

Step 4: Designing and distributing the questionnaire

The questionnaire design phase of an experiment follows the same procedures and guidelines as those given for a survey in Chapter 5. Aside from the manipulations, all other variables should be measured as they would be in a survey, with a focus on ensuring that the measurements are valid. The questions in the questionnaire should also roughly follow the same order as presented in Chapter 5, with a few adjustments to incorporate the manipulation, as illustrated in Textbox 7.1.

Textbox 7.1 Standard order for experiment questionnaires

1. Screener questions that qualify participants for the survey
2. Manipulation of independent variable(s)
3. Measure of dependent variable
4. Measures of mediator variables – in reverse order if it is a serial mediation
5. Measures of moderator variables
6. Manipulation checks
7. Demographic variables

Control variables are not typically included in experiments due to the ability to control for alternative explanations experimentally rather than statistically, but if it is desirable to include control variables, they should be measured after manipulation checks and before demographics.

As mentioned earlier, for experiments that are run online or computerized, questionnaires can be created using survey software such as Qualtrics or SurveyMonkey. These software platforms enable the researcher to randomly assign qualified participants to different conditions of the independent variable and to display only the relevant manipulation. For example, in Qualtrics this can be accomplished through the survey flow feature. If the experiment is not being run on a computer but the manipulation is incorporated into the questionnaire, different versions of the questionnaire can be printed and distributed based on the random assignment of participants to conditions. If the questionnaire is separate from the manipulation, as in the music manipulation in Loureiro, Roschk and Lima (2019) or the manipulation of the invitation mailing in Peck and Johnson (2011), then the questionnaire can be identical for all participants. There may also be some field experiments in which the dependent variable is collected directly, and a questionnaire is not necessary, as in the jazz club experiment in Cui and Wiggins (2017).

The remaining decisions related to distributing the questionnaire follow the same guidelines as presented in Chapter 5.

Step 5: Analyzing and presenting the data

Experimental data is almost always analyzed with analysis of variance or ANOVA, a version of the general linear model in which the independent variables are categorical rather than continuous. A one-factor, two-level design can be tested with an independent samples t-test, a simplified version of a one-way ANOVA. This tests whether the mean responses on the dependent variable among participants within each condition are statistically different. A statistically significant result indicates that the difference between the two group means represents an underlying difference in response patterns and is not simply due to chance. Note that this does not necessarily indicate that the mean difference is substantively significant. It is important to examine the values of the two means and the distance between them to determine if the finding is consistent with the hypothesized effect and large enough to be interesting.

A one-factor design with more than two levels can also be analyzed with a one-way ANOVA. A significant F-test indicates that at least one of the conditions is different from at least one other condition. To further explore the differences across conditions, post hoc contrasts or pairwise comparisons should be run to compare each condition to the others. This can be done manually or through a single test that controls for the overall error rate, such as a Bonferroni or Tukey test. For more information on these tests, see Chapter 8 in Grimm and Yarnold (1994). Specific contrasts may also be planned ahead of time, for example, in a nested design it is common to plan to compare each of the treatment conditions to the control condition. Table 7.1 illustrates the output for an ANOVA with pairwise comparisons.

While the execution of a 2 x 2 factorial design is similar to that of a one-factor design, the analysis is different. A factorial design should not be analyzed using a one-way ANOVA to compare the conditions to each other. Rather, each manipulated variable or factor should be entered into the ANOVA separately in order to test the main effect of the first variable, the main effect of the second variable, and the interaction between the two, which is most likely the result of interest to the researcher. If one of the variables in the factorial design has more than two conditions, contrasts or pairwise comparisons are again appropriate to test which conditions are significantly different, as discussed previously. Table 7.2 illustrates the output for a 2 x 2 ANOVA.

Table 7.1 Example of ANOVA output for a one-factor, four-level design with pairwise comparisons

ANOVA

Source	Type III Sum of Squares	Degrees of Freedom	Mean Square	F	p
Intercept	4975.734	1	4975.734	10046.371	<.001
Condition	6.809	3	2.27	4.583	.004
Error	182.262	368	.495		
Total	5173.552	372			

Pairwise Comparisons

(i) Condition	(j) Condition	Mean Difference	Standard Error	p
1	2	.273*	.104	.009
	3	–.036	.103	.726
	4	.226*	.103	.028
2	1	–.273*	.104	.009
	3	–.309*	.104	.003
	4	–.047	.104	.651
3	1	.036	.103	.726
	2	.309*	.104	.003
	4	.262*	.102	.011
4	1	–.226*	.103	.028
	2	.047	.104	.651
	3	–.262*	.102	.011

If control variables are included in the experiment, you may wish to run an ANCOVA, or analysis of covariance, which enables you to enter control variables into the equation similar to the way you would in regression analysis. The output will show the same main and interaction effects as in an ANOVA, but the results will account for the effects of the control variable. ANCOVA is also sometimes used to test a measured moderator, but it is better to test for an interaction between a manipulated independent variable and a measured moderator using the PROCESS macro in SPSS.

If your design includes a within-subjects variable, it should be analyzed using a Repeated Measures ANOVA, an analysis of variance that accounts for the same participant completing the same measure at more than one time point. The output will again look the same, but the results for the with-

Table 7.2 Example of ANOVA output for a 2 x 2 factorial design

ANOVA					
Source	**Type III Sum of Squares**	**Degrees of Freedom**	**Mean Square**	**F**	**p**
Intercept	4975.734	1	4975.734	10046.371	<.001
Factor 1	.160	1	.160	.323	.570
Factor 2	6.672	1	6.672	13.471	<.001
Factor 1 x Factor 2	.003	1	.003	.06	.940
Error	182.262	368	.495		
Total	5173.552	372			

in-subjects variable should be interpreted as a significant change in participants' responses over time, as opposed to a significant difference across groups. Repeated Measures ANOVA can also incorporate mixed designs, in which case the output will show a test of the change over time of the within-subjects variable, the difference across groups for the between-subjects variable, and the interaction of the two.

Finally, if you are measuring multiple dependent variables that are expected to be correlated with each other, such as attitude towards the organization and behavioral intentions toward the organization, the correct analysis would be a multivariate analysis of variance or a MANOVA. This analysis provides an initial overall analysis of the effect of the independent variable(s) on the set of dependent variables, accounting for the correlation between the dependent variables. If this overall F-test is significant, this indicates that the independent variable(s) have an effect on at least one of the dependent variables. This is followed by univariate analyses for each dependent variable as you would see in a standard ANOVA.

Presentation of experimental results usually begins with a description of the sample demographics and relevant characteristics, followed by tests of the specific hypothesized effects. ANOVA results are typically presented with the main effects of each independent variable followed by a statement that these effects are qualified by a significant interaction effect. If the main effects are not significant, the statement is phrased as neither independent variable having a main effect but the interaction effect being significant. Statistics for each effect are presented in parentheses, including the group means, F- or t-statistic, and p-value. If contrasts have been run, they are

Table 7.3 Sample presentation of experimental results in a table Peck and Johnson (2011)

	Low Autotelic NFT		High Autotelic NFT	
Persuasion Measures	**Neutral Haptic (Paper Band) $n = 190$**	**Positive Haptic (Velvet Band) $n = 201$**	**Neutral Haptic (Paper Band) $n = 199$**	**Positive Haptic (Velvet Band) $n = 207$**
Attitude toward the brochure (means and standard deviations)	5.12 (1.57)	4.86 (1.63)	5.22[a] (1.47)	5.49[a] (1.30)
Likelihood of attending the Viennese Ball	1.63 (1.43)	1.69 (1.54)	1.91 (1.76)	1.82 (1.65)

Note: Numbers with same superscript within autotelic NFT condition are significantly different, $p < 0.05$.

presented after the relevant main or interaction effects, with an indication of whether they were run as post hoc or planned contrasts and the specific test that was run if relevant.

Experimental results are also commonly presented in table form, as in the example illustrated in Table 7.3.

Results can also be presented in graphical form, as in the example illustrated in Figure 7.8.

As with survey research, the questionnaire is not typically presented; however, it is common to present images of the manipulations, if relevant, and a list of measures with their reliabilities. For more detail on presenting measures, see this section in Chapter 5.

Conclusion

Experiments are a powerful research tool due to their ability to test for causal relationships between variables. It is important to remember the three criteria necessary for testing cause: 1) manipulation of the independent variable, 2) random assignment of participants to conditions, and 3) control of situational factors that could provide alternative explanations for the results. These three elements are key to the effective design of an experiment. In practice, they can be successfully executed through careful attention to the design and pretesting of manipulations, the use of computerized randomization tools (or even simple randomization tools such as assigning each person who arrives at the research lab to condition 1 and condition 2 in an alternating pattern), and careful control of the situation to ensure

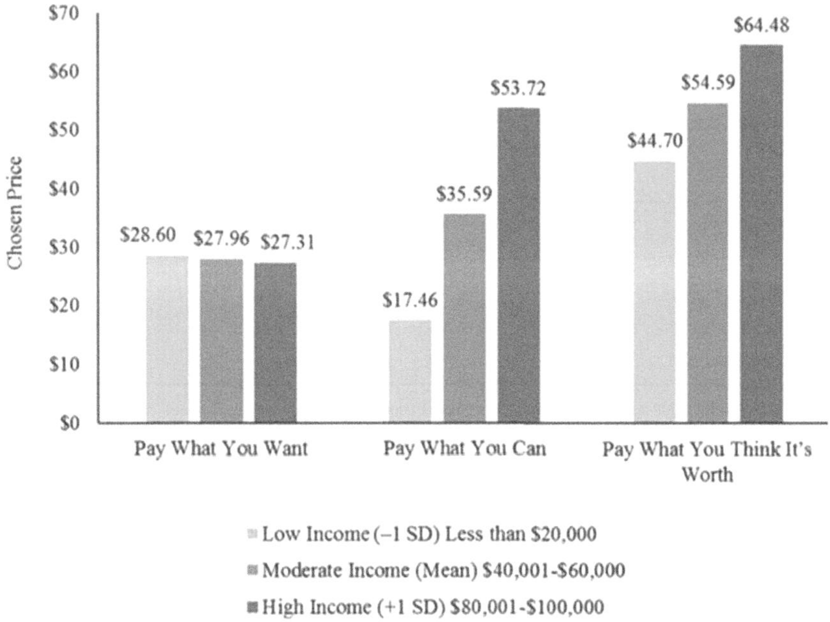

Figure 7.8 Sample presentation of experimental results in graphical form
Source: Cui and Wiggins (2017)

that participants' experience outside of the manipulation is as identical as possible.

While a true experiment is the best way to meet these three criteria, there are often reasons to value realism and generalizability, or external validity, over tight experimental control, or internal validity. For this reason, researchers often use a combination of laboratory and field experiments to test a hypothesis, taking advantage of the benefits of both experimental types. This can also be accomplished in a mixed methods design that pairs experiments with analysis of secondary data from the field. In addition, the need to isolate a particular causal effect in order to test a hypothesis means that experiments typically contain fewer variables than other forms of quantitative research. To test a complex model, especially one containing multiple moderating effects, researchers often design a series of experiments to test different parts of the model. These concerns imply that experimental researchers should expect to conduct and present a series of studies, not a single study, in order to fully test their theory. A series of well-designed experiments that balance the need for experimental control with the need for realism and generalizability can provide strong evidence supporting a causal effect.

References

Baumgarth, C., & Bahati Wieker, J. (2020), "From the classical art to the urban art infusion effect: The effect of street art and graffiti on the consumer evaluation of products," *Creativity and Innovation Management*, 29(S1), 116–127.

Broekman van Mourik, A., Koudenburg, N., Gordijn, E. H., Krans, K. L. S., & Postmes, T. (2019), "The impact of art: Exploring the social-psychological pathways that connect audiences to live performances," *Journal of Personality and Social Psychology: Interpersonal Relations and Group Processes*, 116(6), 942–965.

Cui, A. P., & Wiggins, J. (2017), "What you ask changes what I pay: Framing effects in pay what you want pricing," *Journal of Marketing Theory and Practice*, 25(4), 323–339.

Grimm, L. G., & Yarnold, P. R. (1994), *Reading and understanding multivariate statistics*. American Psychological Association.

Hale, J. S., & Woronkowicz, J. (2019), "Evaluating a university's investment in arts programming on student arts participation," *Cultural Trends*, 28(5), 366–378.

Hernando, E., & Campo, S. (2017), "Does the artist's name influence the perceived value of an artwork?," *International Journal of Arts Management*, 19(2), 46–58.

Hoffmann, R., & Coate, B. (2022), "Fame, what's your name? Quasi and statistical gender discrimination in an art valuation experiment," *Journal of Economic Behavior and Organization*, 202, 184–197.

Johnson, J. W., & Peng Cui, A. (2013), "To influence or not to influence: External reference price strategies in pay-what-you-want pricing," *Journal of Business Research*, 66(2), 275–281.

Joye, Y., & Fennis, B. M. (2024), "Set that record straight! Cardinal line orientations in music album artwork boost market performance and music consumption," *Psychology & Marketing*, 41, 916–937.

Loureiro, S. M. C., Roschk, H., & Lima, F. (2019), "The role of background music in visitors' experience of art exhibitions: Music, memory and art appraisal," *International Journal of Arts Management*, 22(1), 4–24.

Peck, J., & Johnson, J. W. (2011), "Autotelic need for touch, haptics and persuasion: The role of involvement," *Psychology & Marketing*, 28(3), 222–239.

Shadish, W. R., Cook, T. D., & Campbell, D. T. (2002), *Experimental and quasi-experimental designs for generalized causal inference*. Belmont, CA: Cengage.

Wang, Y., Jing Xu, A., & Zhang, Y. (2022), "*L'art pour l'art*: Experiencing art reduces the desire for luxury goods," *Journal of Consumer Research*, 39, 786–810.

Wiggins, J. (2018), "Can consumers perceive collective psychological ownership of an organization?," in J. Peck, & S. Shu (Eds.), *Psychological ownership and consumer behavior* (pp. 177–194). Cham, Switzerland: Springer International Publishing.

Wiggins, J., Song, C., Trivedi, D., & Preece, S. B. (2017), "Consumer perceptions of arts organizations' strategies for responding to critique," *International Journal of Arts Management*, 20(1), 4–20.

8

CASE STUDIES

Introduction

Case studies offer a unique opportunity for understanding complex phenomena within their real-world contexts. This chapter explores the methodological underpinnings, practical applications, and challenges of using case studies as a research method in culture and arts management. It outlines the principles of case study research, emphasizing its role in theory development, and provides valuable advice for novice researchers. Drawing extensively on Yin (2014) and Eisenhardt's (1989, 2021) contributions and other seminal works, the chapter focuses on the relevance of case studies for addressing critical "how" and "why" questions in the arts and cultural sectors. By using Eisenhardt (1989, 2021) and Yin (2014) as the principal theorists, it offers a more structured approach to the case studies. However, less structured approaches to case study design also exist, and readers interested in these perspectives may wish to delve into authors such as Stake (1995, 2005).

What is case study?

A case study is a research method focused on a deep, contextual analysis of a particular situation. Although many authors often consider it to be a qualitative method, it may encompass quantitative data analysis. Interestingly, Eisenhardt (1989) refers to case studies as "a research strategy", not

 DOI: 10.4324/9781003487951-8

an approach or a method. The case(s) itself can be structured around one or many different instances such as, but not limited to, organizations (i.e. a museum), events (i.e. the arrival of a new artistic director; an exposition), projects (i.e. a fundraising campaign), individuals (i.e. an artist), or even a combination of these entities, provided it represents a bounded system of interest. "Bounded system of interest" means that the object of study must be clearly defined. It can be done by, for instance, identifying a specific time period, the actors or stakeholders to be analyzed, a set of events, and their consequences. Yin (2003, 2014) defines case studies as empirical inquiries investigating contemporary phenomena ("the case") in depth within real-life contexts, especially when boundaries between the phenomena and the context may not be clearly evident. He goes further (Yin, 2014) and adds three other features to case studies: they (1) cope with the technically distinctive situation in which there will be many more variables of interest than data points, and as one result (2) rely on multiple sources of evidence, with data needing to converge in a triangulating fashion, and as another result (3) benefit from the prior development of theoretical propositions to guide data collection and analysis (p. 17). As you will see, triangulation refers to the combination of multiple data sources to corroborate/compare findings and minimize bias.

From a managerial perspective, case studies are particularly useful in arts management research because the cultural field is full of complex situations stemming from its specificities. Our organizations, very frequently, are co-led by artistic directors and CEOs and our products, the artistic product, are often created before any market analysis. From a conceptual standpoint, these rich situations constitute great opportunities for theory development and for a deep understanding of complex managerial challenges.

Of course, as we have seen in Chapters 2, 3, and 4, every research project starts with ethical clearance, a thorough literature review and the identification of a clear research question. The way we set the research question influences the type of method we choose. As we will see, case studies are usually a good option to answer questions such as "how" or "why." Also, if a researcher wishes to perform a deeper description and analysis of a complex situation, the case study method will be very useful. For example, Rentschler, Lee and Fillis (2021) chose a longitudinal case study – meaning that data were collected across different points over time – to explore the scenario of an Australian regional museum before, during and after a governance crisis.

With no doubt, this is a complex situation that demands in-depth analysis. The problem involved different stakeholders (board members and staff), different time periods (before, during, and after the crisis) and multiple data sources (reports, interviews, websites, and internal documents). The richness of this data, as much as it offers an opportunity for a multi-level and diverse analysis, also represents a challenge in terms of the amount of information to be examined. To make sense of this high volume of data, the authors drew on three theories of governance to guide their work: agency theory, stewardship theory, and stakeholder theory (Rentschler, Lee & Fillis, 2021). As a result, they show how the integration of different governance-related theoretical approaches can help managers face periods of crisis.

It is important to note that a research case study is different from a teaching case study. The latter is a pedagogical document, mostly descriptive, for classroom usage (for an example see Dantas et al., 2024). The former is a research endeavor where a theoretical contribution is the main objective, using a single case study (see for example Rentschler, Lee & Subramaniam, 2023) or multi-case studies (see for example Donelli et al., 2023). While the mere description of a situation can be extremely valuable in some contexts such as the identification of best practices, when it comes to academic research we need to go beyond a simple description. As we saw in the previous paragraph, a good indicator of the academic scope of a case study is the possibility to apply its conclusions to theory and in other scenarios. Research case studies entail some level of theoretical analysis, going beyond a mere description of facts. For instance, to understand the impact of the live music scene in the branding of a city, Baiocchi et al. (2024) adopted a multi-case study. They compared the cases of Montreal, Canada, and Rio de Janeiro, Brazil, to understand how the cultural identity and the infrastructure of these cities interact and impact the image of the place. While the data were collected geographically bounded, the results are generalized to other cities. This chapter focuses on research case studies.

When to use case studies as a research method?

Case studies can be chosen as the only method in a research project (i.e. Fillis & Lee, 2011; Kottasz et al., 2007) or be one among many in multi-method studies (i.e. Jancovich, 2015). The research objectives and research question determine the final methodological toolset to be adopted and the role (main or secondary) that the case study takes in the research, as we saw in Chapter 2. As Yin (2003) explains, "the case study is the method of choice when the phenomenon under study is not readily distinguishable from its context" (p. 4). Indeed, the context is essential when using case studies in academic research projects.

Take, for instance, the research by Crepaz, Huber and Scheytt (2016) about the role of the state (or government) as a network actor. They chose the single case of the European Capital of Culture and showed, through the analysis of complex practices of valuation, how the state "influences artistic and arts management processes" (p. 47). Hence, had they chosen a case outside the arts and culture world and, more importantly, without the complexities of the European Capital of Culture these researchers would not arrive to the same conclusions such as that the actors involved in this initiative "use the state and 'its interests' as a discursive resource in order to influence economic decisions (and thereby indirectly artistic ones)" (p. 48). However, even though the context is intrinsically related to the phenomenon under study, it is important to note that the conclusions should still apply to theory and potentially other scenarios.

The reader must note that there are different types of case studies, and the literature in management proposes different typologies regarding them. Thomas (2011), for instance, suggests a typology based on the following layers: subject and object, purpose, approach, and process of the case study. The *subject* is the specific case or instance at study. It is the "practical, historical unity" selected for its capacity to reveal insights about the object. The subject is not representative of a wider population but is chosen for its uniqueness, interest, or relevance to the study. Examples might include a particular event, institution, or social phenomenon. Subjects can be local (easy-access or familiar cases), key (cases that are particularly illustrative of a situation) or outlier cases (extreme, unusual, or exceptional situations). *Objects*, in turn, refer to the analytical or theoretical frame that defines the lens through which the *subject* is examined. For instance, while the subject might be a specific theater festival, the *object* could be the broader concept of "creation of ephemeral artistic products" or "the management of temporary workers". While the *subject* is specific, context-bounded, the *object* is more general. The *purpose* describes the reason for conducting the case study (i.e. analyzing the case for its own sake due to its inherent interest or understanding a broader issue or phenomenon, etc.). The *approach* relates to the methodological choice and theoretical orientation of the study. Here, we can find theory-building (i.e. when you are proposing a new theory, or a new explanation to a phenomenon), theory-testing (i.e. when you are, for example, testing existing theories in a new setting) or descriptive cases (i.e. when you are simply describing a situation, without worrying about building or testing theory). Finally, the *process* relates to the operational structure of the case study, including how data are collected and analyzed over time. The different combinations of these layers create different types of cases. Other authors have proposed other typologies (you can refer, for instance, to Baxter and Jack (2008) or Eisenhardt (2021) for some examples). Since the description of different types of case studies are not the focus of this chapter, the rest of this chapter concentrates on the different stages related to the completion of a research case study.

Key stages in case study research

There is a vast literature about the case study approach in management. For those interested in diving deeper in this topic, here are two suggested starting points. First, if your main objective is theory-building, take a look at Kathleen Eisenhardt's work (1989, 2021) in which she explains how to build new theories from case studies and on the work of Ann Langley (Langley, 2009; Langley et al., 2013) for a processual view of this type of research. Second, for a more general description of the method, including projects focused mostly on managerial challenges, consult Robert Yin's book (2014). There are five key stages related to case study research.

Step 1: Define a research question

A research question forms the foundation of any case study. Its purpose is to guide the focus of the inquiry, to set some boundaries to the exploration, while remaining flexible to adapt as new insights emerge during the research process. Yin (2014) highlights that the evolutionary nature of the research question is one of the distinctive characteristics and strengths of case studies.

For example, a researcher might start with a question such as, "What factors influence the success of community-based art initiatives?" As data are gathered and analyzed, the question might evolve to "How do local partnerships contribute to the longevity of these initiatives?" This flexibility is critical in arts management research, especially in qualitative studies, where dynamic factors such as audience engagement, funding, and cultural trends come into play. As we will see, data analysis and data collection occurring simultaneously enables the research question to be adjusted along the way.

Here, it is important to note that the research question should not be focused on studying festival X or museum Y specifically. While you might find it interesting to explore some aspects of these institutions, the choice of the context in which you conduct your research should come after you decide on your research question.

When crafting a research question, remember that it must, in general, emphasize exploratory analysis. The question should be specific enough to guide the research and the identification of data sources and key informants, but broad enough to accommodate unexpected (and interesting!) findings. However, as Baxter and Jack (2008) highlight, "one of the common pitfalls associated with case study is that there is a tendency for researchers to attempt to answer a question that is too broad or a topic that has too many objectives for one study" (p. 546). Hence, it is important to define boundaries around the case by identifying, for instance, one or more organizations, individuals, events, phenomena, or time periods that are at the core of the researcher's interest. This is the object of step 2.

Step 2: Determine the subject and set the boundaries

Once you have decided what will be your research question, it is time to specify the boundaries of the research, such as its *subject*. As we saw earlier, the *subject* is the specific case at study. This is the first level of delimitation that needs to be chosen. Baxter and Jack (2008) propose a series of questions to identify the "case": "do I want to 'analyze' the individual? Do I want to 'analyze' a program? Do I want to 'analyze the process? Do I want to 'analyze' the difference between organizations?" (page 545)

For example, if you want to explore how local partnerships contribute to longevity of community-based art initiatives (CBAI), your "case" (or unit of analysis) could be, for instance, the different local partnerships that one or many of such art initiatives have developed over the last years.

Once you have identified the unit of analysis, you need to identify the context in which the research will take place. You will need to provide a rationale as to why that context was chosen and how the boundaries around it were determined. Will you focus on a time period (the last 10 years)? An industry (the book editing industry in your country)? A specific actor (artistic directors)? Baxter and Jack (2008) call this "bind[ing] the case". Defining, or "binding", the case will help ensure your study remains manageable in scope. These boundaries clarify what aspects will be included or excluded in the research project.

For example, if my *subjects* are the local partnerships related to community-based arts initiatives, I must build a list of all types of companies and individuals that have collaborated with the community-based arts initiative(s) that is(are) the focus of my case study. Then, I might decide, for instance, that I will only concentrate on partnerships featuring companies, not individuals. This decision can be based on theoretical or conceptual reasons but also on practical issues, such as the sample size or the access to data and respondents. As Eisenhardt (1989) highlights, in situations in which we seek to build theory from case studies, random selection of cases (or *subjects*) is not necessary – "the goal of theoretical sampling is to choose cases which are likely to replicate or extend the emergent theory" (p. 537). The result of this process might be, for example, the choice of a specific longstanding local festival of street art, which might feature different types of partnerships with local companies that eventually could explain the longevity of such a festival.

Then you need to consider what type of case study will be undertaken. The overall goal of your research will guide the selection of a particular type of case study design. The choice of cases – or *subjects* – impacts the reliability and validity (for quantitative studies), richness, trustworthiness and authenticity (for qualitative studies), and theoretical contributions of the research. Here, one of the most important decisions to make is if you will conduct a single or a multiple case study. A single case might explore how one CBAI has build its partnerships with individuals and how it impacts its longevity, while a multiple case study might compare how different CBAIs have done it. In the case of multiple cases, the choice of subjects might be driven by an interest to show very different strategies (i.e. to show contrast) or a clear trend. One advantage of running a single case study is that the researcher is able to dive deeper into the phenomenon at study: instead of having a single respondent per organization, it is possible, for instance, to interview the managers, the staff, some clients, visitors, etc., and add other sources of information to the data analysis.

Another way of limiting the scope of the case study and keeping it more focused is to create a set of theoretical propositions or theoretical frameworks that the researchers wish to explore. This relates to the *object* of the case study, as we saw earlier. These propositions direct data collection, determine the scope of the research, and form the foundation for a conceptual framework. They are derived mostly from the literature but could also come from the personal experience of researchers. It is important to note that while this could be extremely helpful, crafting propositions might not be necessary in some types of cases studies especially when the creation of new theories is not the main goal of the research.

For example, one simple proposition regarding partnerships might state that mutual benefits in partnerships are the drivers of the longevity of a CBAI. Of course, this type of proposition must be crafted based on previous literature, which will indicate possible theoretical explanations for the phenomenon under study, helping the researcher to identify areas that have been overlooked by previous studies.

Step 3: Craft and test the tools

Data collection in case study research involves gathering information from multiple sources to ensure a comprehensive understanding of the phenomenon under investigation. As Yin highlights, this is one of the strengths of case studies: the opportunity to use many different sources of evidence. The diversity of information sources allows us to address a wider scope of historical (archival data, internal reports, previous research) and behavioral (interviews and field observations) information (Yin, 2014). Table 8.1 shows examples of six different sources of evidence.

The development of data collection instruments and protocols is a critical component of any case study research process, ensuring consistency in data collection and analysis, reliability, trustworthiness, authenticity, and credibility of findings. Well-designed instruments facilitate the systematic gathering of data relevant to the research objectives, while protocols establish uniformity in their application. Eisenhardt (1989) stresses the importance of employing multiple methods to strengthen data triangulation and enhance the validity of research outcomes.

The process of crafting data collection instruments involves several steps to warrant their effectiveness and reliability. First, it is essential to define clear objectives, ensuring that the instruments are specifically designed to capture data directly aligned with the research questions and propositions. Since each case study is unique in relation to its scope and final objectives, they require specific tools. In some cases, depth interviews – conducted

Table 8.1 Seven different sources of evidence

Source of evidence	Examples
Documentation	Administrative documents, formal studies, letters, e-mails, diaries, news clippings, agendas, etc.
Archival records	Secondary data such as census reports, internal data not necessarily structured in reports, past budgets, maps, survey data, etc.
Interviews	Individual interviews, either with open-ended questions using interview guides or structured survey questionnaires.
Direct observation	Data generated from structured observation guides or from more informal, or unstructured, observations occurring while collecting other types of data.
Participant-observation	Situations in which the researcher assumes some kind of role in the research setting (voluntary worker for a museum, spectator in a music festival, staff member in an art gallery, member of the board, etc.) in which he or she has the opportunity to adopt a privileged observation point.
Physical artifacts	A tangible work of art, a music instrument, a machine, work tools, personal items, etc.
Virtual artifacts	Websites, intangible works of art (holograms, video projections, illuminations, etc.), mobile applications, software in general.

Source: adapted and extended from Yin (2014)

using interview guides – will be enough. In other situations, these interviews need to be coupled with observation grids and document analysis templates. Both qualitative and quantitative tools can be used in a case study. As we saw in Chapter 6, interview guides typically consist of open-ended questions designed to elicit detailed insights into participants' experiences and perspectives. Observation checklists enable researchers to systematically record behaviors, interactions, or processes during events, meetings, or other activities such as any participation to a cultural activity (installations, immersive experiences, illuminations, concerts, museum visits, etc.). Document analysis templates offer a structured framework for reviewing organizational records, reports, or marketing materials, ensuring a comprehensive and consistent approach to data analysis.

Next, pilot testing serves as a vital step to refine these instruments, allowing researchers to identify ambiguities, address potential biases, and improve overall clarity. It is possible, for instance, to conduct a pilot case study to test the data collection tools (i.e. Rashid et al., 2019). Finally, standardization is necessary to establish protocols that ensure uniformity in data collection across different cases, thereby minimizing variability caused by procedural differences and enhancing the consistency of the research process. This is particularly important with multiple case studies in which we collect data in different organizations, when we collect data in different points in time (for longitudinal case studies) or when different people are simultaneously responsible for the data collection. Once we have crafted the data collection tools, we can start the field work.

Step 4: Collect data

As we just saw, data collection in case study research involves gathering information from multiple sources to ensure a comprehensive understanding of the phenomenon under investigation. As Yin (2014) highlights, this is one of the strengths of case studies: the opportunity to use many different sources of evidence. The multiplicity of sources of evidence allows us to cover a broader range of historical and behavioral elements (Yin, 2014). While this constitutes an amazing source of rich information, different data sources and types of data collection techniques will require a more diverse set of skills from the researcher. Being a good interviewer is different from being able to properly analyze archival data. Hence, before entering the field, you must ensure that you and your team have the necessary expertise to collect and analyze the data associated with your case study. In this sense, partnering with people who can complement you in terms of data collection expertise might be a good idea.

Before moving forward with this discussion, it is important to take a moment to consider two important aspects of every research project: access and ethics (see also Chapter 3). Let's say that you run a thorough literature review and are able to identify an interesting research question, a novel phenomenon in arts management, and an organization that constitutes a unique opportunity to study this phenomenon. All this previous work can be lost if this organization does not grant you access to the data. To prevent this, it is essential to ensure that you have formal permission to collect the data you need, as unauthorized access can jeopardize both your research and the trust of stakeholders. Be explicit about the types of data you intend to collect and how you plan to use it, as clarity fosters transparency and builds confidence with the organization. Furthermore, explicitly define what types of data you will publish, whether verbatim quotes, statistical summaries, anonymous or non-anonymous information, so that all parties are aware of the potential outputs of your study. It is also crucial that the management of the organization communicates with and informs every individual you wish to contact, interview, or observe, ensuring there are no misunderstandings or breaches of trust. If your institution requires signed ethics forms as part of the research process, make sure these are completed and approved before you begin collecting data. These steps not only safeguard the integrity of your research but also demonstrate respect for the participants and the ethical standards of academic inquiry.

Yin (2014) proposes four principles relating to data collection: (1) use multiple sources of evidence, (2) create a case study database, (3) maintain a chain of evidence, and (4) exercise care when using data from electronic sources. They help researchers establish the reliability and the validity of the data collected. This chapter next delves into the first two of these principles.

Principle 1: Use multiple sources of evidence

We use multiple sources of evidence in case studies in order to triangulate the data. Triangulation is a key strategy in case study research, combining data from multiple sources to corroborate findings and minimize bias. It means that you will compare the data and findings coming from different organizations, different data collections, different sources within one organization, different informants, or even different points in time in order to identify consistencies and contradictions. In the case you find consistencies among different data sources, you increase the reliability of these findings. For example, if all voluntary workers and visitors of a CBAI mention the importance of a particular partner in the success of this endeavor, this a great indication that this is a consistent finding. However, if your different informants say opposite things about this partner you might want to add other sources of information to explore this issue or come to the conclusion that different stakeholders have different opinions about the issue at study. This could constitute a very interesting insight. Hence, triangulation is only possible if you have at least two different sources of information. As stated before, the multiplicity of sources is one of the strengths of case studies. Along with securing multiple sources of information, the researcher must, as highlighted earlier, ensure that all data collection tools have been properly developed.

Principle 2: Create a case study database

As you can imagine, with the multiplicity of sources comes the sheer volume of information. This principle deals with the storage, organization, and referencing of the data collected. Since the nature of the information collected can be extremely diverse (from videos to handwritten notes and financial reports), it is essential to determine a strategy to manage the dataset. It is not the objective here to suggest one specific tool, such as data management software, since every case study is unique in terms of its objectives and the type and volume of data that it contains. With the evolution of artificial intelligence tools, the management of large amounts of diverse data is also becoming easier and more accessible.

Since depth interviews are one of the most popular types of data collection in case study research, much of the data management that will take place in case studies is very similar to what was discussed in Chapter 6. However, what is new here is that new sources and types of data will coexist with the transcripts of interviews. The main objective of your data management strategy will be to have all these documents easily retrievable.

In this sense, protocols and note taking are two accessible strategies that you might want to adopt. Regarding note taking, it requires a great deal of discipline from the researcher. It consists of writing down your thoughts, insights, main conclusions, etc., during and after each data collection session. For example, if you participate in an observation of an art exposition, you should take notes during the event to document what you see (behaviors, discussions, artworks, etc.) and immediately after the exposition to record your impressions, conclusions, relationships to other observations/interviews and, most importantly, to your theoretical propositions. These are also called field notes. Later in the process, you can review these notes, compare them and, if necessary, go back to the original data or transcripts to validate your conclusions. One of the advantages of using notes is to summarize the information and, hence, accelerate the analysis process. Miles and Huberman (1994) offer thorough presentation of different methods and techniques on how to analyze and present qualitative data.

Protocols will help you to have clear procedures for data collection and analysis. They are the blueprint of the research project. A protocol is directed to the researchers (not the participants!) and contains the overview of the case study (goals, main questions), the data collection procedures (types of organizations or individuals to be interviewed, how, where and for how long to store the information collected, tasks to be completed prior to and after the fieldwork, etc.) and the roles of each team member. The most important thing here is not the format that the protocol will take, but the fact that all researchers involved in the project discuss these issues and remain aware of them the whole time.

Step 5: Analyze the data

A unique feature of case studies is that the data collection and the data analysis very frequently occur simultaneously. A typical example is what was described earlier regarding field notes: the researchers, immediately after collecting fresh data, start to reflect on the possible learning points and conclusions to be taken. As Eisenhardt (1989, p. 539) puts it, "overlapping data analysis with data collection not only gives the researcher a head start in analysis but, more importantly, allows researchers to take advantage of flexible data collection". This back-and-forth between data collection and analysis might also allow researchers to adjust their data collection instruments and eventually identify new sources of data to consider.

Analysis is inherently cyclical, involving a dynamic interplay between data and conclusions, where findings are continuously revisited and refined. Eisenhardt (1989), for instance, suggests a few strategies to analyze case study data. One of these strategies is within-case analysis, which typically involves detailed case study write-ups for each organization or element that constitutes the case at study. The idea here is to have a detailed description of the exploration of each organization to generate first insights and conclusions. Having this first round of analysis in an isolated mode, meaning that we make no comparisons between cases, allows us to identify features that are related to the unique characteristics of the case study. A natural next step would be to "expand" the analysis to look for similarities and differences between elements. As the analysis progresses, researchers can employ various tactics to enhance the depth and richness of their findings. Another approach consists of identifying specific dimensions or themes and analyzing both the similarities and the differences in the data from different sources, facilitating a structured analysis. The identification of these dimensions must be related to the research question and the theoretical propositions of the case study. To that matter, Yin (2014) underscores the necessity of linking data to theoretical propositions in order to strengthen the study's theoretical grounding. Returning to the original propositions during analysis is a crucial practice. This process helps maintain analytical focus, preventing the inclusion of data that fall outside the study's scope. Furthermore, considering rival propositions creates an opportunity to explore alternative explanations for the phenomenon under investigation. Engaging in this iterative approach strengthens confidence in the findings, as each proposition and its potential counterarguments are systematically examined, accepted, or rejected (Baxter & Jack, 2008). Finally, another strategy involves dividing the data by source, with different researchers focusing on distinct types of data – such as observations, interviews, and questionnaire responses – ensuring a comprehensive and multi-faceted analysis.

Content analysis is often used in case studies, providing rigor in data that can be triangulated with other means, such as interviews or observations, for example. It is defined as "a research technique for making replicable and valid inferences from text (or other meaningful matter) to the contexts of their use" (Krippendorff, 2019, p. 24). Content analysis may take different forms and requires a rigorous approach by the researcher. Properly covering all its aspects is beyond of the scope of this chapter. Those interested in learning more about this technique are invited to explore the work of Krippendorff (2019).

In the end, the type of data and the research objectives will determine the data analysis strategy that is the most appropriate to your project. The most important thing is to seek rigor and transparency. Readers of your work should be able to clearly identify the methods you employ and the reasons behind your methodological choices. Chapter 10 explores more about how to present and write the findings of your research.

Conclusion

Case studies provide unparalleled insight into complex, real-world phenomena. For early-career arts management scholars, they provide a versatile tool for exploring, describing, and explaining the intricacies of issues related to policy and evaluation; the governance and management of cultural organizations; the study of individuals who work in them and work independently of them; and the consumption of artistic products. By adhering to methodological rigor, scholars can contribute to both theoretical advances and practical solutions. This chapter has highlighted the importance of defining clear research questions, selecting appropriate cases, and employing multiple sources of evidence to ensure a robust and comprehensive analysis.

Furthermore, it explored the iterative nature of case study research, where data collection and analysis occur simultaneously in a dynamic process that allows for continuous refinement of insights and theoretical propositions. Various analytical strategies, such as within-case and cross-case analyses, pattern matching, and thematic coding, were presented as essential tools for structuring and interpreting case study data. Additionally, this chapter underscored the ethical considerations associated with case study research, including the necessity of obtaining ethical clearance, formal permission from your university as well as your participants and or their organization, ensuring transparency in data use, and adhering to ethical guidelines when working with participants. Ultimately, this chapter has provided a framework for conducting rigorous case study research, equipping researchers with the methodological tools necessary to navigate the complexities of studying the arts and cultural ecosystem, including government departments, businesses and organizations, and individuals.

References

Baiocchi, A., Dantas, D. C., Pessôa, L. A. G. P., & Colbert, F. (2024), "Cultural branding of cities: The role of live music in building a city's brand," *Cultural Trends*, 1–19.

Baxter, P., & Jack, S. (2008), "Qualitative case study methodology: Study design and implementation for novice researchers," *The Qualitative Report*, 13(4), 544–559.

Crepaz, L., Huber, C., & Scheytt, T. (2016), "Governing arts through valuation: The role of the state as network actor in the European Capital of Culture 2010," *Critical Perspectives on Accounting*, 37, 35–50.

Dantas, D. C., Carvalho, A., Correia Dubeux, V. J., & Mansur, B. (2024), "Partnerships between artists and brands: A case study in the Brazilian music market," *International Journal of Arts Management*, 26(3), 80–87.

Donelli, C. C., Rentschler, R., Fanelli, S., & Lee, B. (2023). "Philanthropy patterns in major Australian performing arts organizations." *Journal of Management and Governance*, 27(4), 1367–1396.

Eisenhardt, K. M. (1989), "Building theories from case study research," *Academy of Management Review*, 14(4), 532–550.

Eisenhardt, K. M. (2021), "What is the Eisenhardt method, really?," *Strategic Organization*, 19(1), 147–160.

Fillis, I., & Lee, B. (2011), "Internationalisation of Korean performing arts: A case study analysis," *European Journal of Marketing*, 45(5), 822–846.

Jancovich, L. (2015), "Breaking down the fourth wall in arts management: The implications of engaging users in decision-making," *International Journal of Arts Management*, 18(1), 14–25.

Kottasz, R., Bennett, R., Savani, S., Mousley, W., & Ali-Choudhury, R. (2007), "The role of the corporate art collection in corporate identity management: The case of Deutsche Bank," *International Journal of Arts Management*, 10(1), 19–31.

Krippendorff, K. (2019), *Content analysis: An introduction to its methodology*. Los Angeles, CA: Sage Publications.

Langley, A. (2009), "Studying processes in and around organizations," in *The Sage handbook of organizational research methods* (pp. 409–429). London: Sage.

Langley, A., Smallman, C., Tsoukas, H., & Van de Ven, A. H. (2013), "Process studies of change in organization and management: Unveiling temporality, activity, and flow," *Academy of Management Journal*, 56(1), 1–13.

Miles, M. B., & Huberman, A. M. (1994), *Qualitative data analysis: An expanded sourcebook.* Thousand Oaks, CA: Sage.

Rashid, Y., Rashid, A., Warraich, M. A., Sabir, S. S., & Waseem, A. (2019), "Case study method: A step-by-step guide for business researchers," *International Journal of Qualitative Methods*, 18, 1–13. https://doi.org/10.1177/1609406919862424.

Rentschler, R., Lee, B., & Fillis, I. (2021), "Towards an integrative framework for arts governance," *International Journal of Arts Management*, 24(1), 17–31.

Rentschler, R., Lee, B., & Subramaniam, N. (2023). "Festival innovation in times of crisis." *Event Management*, 27(4), 559–575.

Stake, R. E. (1995), *The art of case study research.* Thousand Oaks, CA: Sage Publications.

Stake, R. E. (2005), *Multiple case study analysis.* New York, NY: The Guilford Press.

Thomas, G. (2011), "A typology for the case study in social science following a review of definition, discourse, and structure," *Qualitative Inquiry*, 17(6), 511–521.

Yin, R. K. (2003), *Applications of case study research* (2nd ed.). Thousand Oaks, CA: Sage Publications. (Applied social research methods series, vol. 34).

Yin, R. K. (2014), *Case study research: Design and methods* (5th ed.). Thousand Oaks, CA: Sage Publications.

9

Ethnography, Netnography, and Observation

Introduction

Ethnography comes from the Greek *ethnos* for a people, group, or culture, and "graphic," meaning writing or representing (Belk, Fischer & Kozinets, 2013). As Hackley (2020, p. 162) emphasizes, ethnography is characterized by four signature features:

1. Use of multiple qualitative data sources
2. Naturalistic focus on everyday behavior
3. Seeking emic insights from direct engagement with small groups
4. Relatively unstructured data gathering in early stages of an iterative process

An *emic* focus means trying to understand things from the participants' point of view, whereas an *etic* understanding, which may come later in an interpretive study, is seeking understanding from an outsider's perspective. Only an insider can reveal what it means, for example, to be an avid fan in hip hop music, while generally only an outsider can reveal how this may differ between the US and the Netherlands and suggest an interpretation of why. The researcher may also be able to detect differences across people within a group – something that group members may not fully appreciate. For instance, even if two people say "I love you" to each other, they may each mean different things by it.

 DOI: 10.4324/9781003487951-9

There are different types of ethnographies, depending mostly on how ethnographic methods are used and what sorts of data they emphasize. The term *netnography* is a mash-up of the terms ethnography and internet, suggesting that the groups studied are considered primarily through their online expressions, postings, and conversations (Kozinets, 2019). A *visual ethnography* tries to understand people through using mostly still images (Pink, 2001). The images can either be interpreted by themselves (images produced by the researcher, the participants, or a third party) or used as stimuli to elicit further reflection by the participants. When the images are used as stimuli the procedure is called *visual elicitation* (Tian & Belk, 2005) or *autodriving* (Heisley & Levy, 1991). When the images (and usually the presentation media) are video or film the method is *videography* (Belk & Kozinets, 2024; Heath, Hindmarsh & Luff, 2010). And when the researcher is the source and focus of the ethnography, it is called *autoethnography* (Zouaoui, 2024). Further, a type of ethnography designed for virtual worlds when the researcher is represented by an avatar is called *immersive netnography* Boellstorff, 2008; Kozinets, 2023). Some would add *critical ethnography* and *virtual ethnography* to this list as well (Angrosino, 2007; Moisander & Valtonen, 2006). These methods all share the four traits listed in the opening paragraph. For purposes of this chapter, we will generally use ethnography as involving some combination of these methods. But we will dive into netnography and observation (including visual ethnography and videography) separately.

Ethnography

This chapter could also contain the depth interview methods discussed in Chapter 6, as these are also critical to conducting an ethnography. So are netnography and observation as discussed in this chapter. Ethnography originated with anthropologists like Bronislaw Malinowsky (1922, 1926), who founded modern anthropology with his work in the Trobriand Islands of Papua New Guinea. His work in the islands from 1916-1918 involved learning the language, intensive observation, careful journaling, and interviews – techniques that are still the backbone of academic anthropology today. However, he lacked modern laptops, cell phones, and the internet, and he utilized "front porch ethnography," in which the natives came to be interviewed by this neo-colonialist at his tent. With careful observation in particular, he revealed complex patterns of gift-giving, agriculture, fishing, farming, and life rituals among those he still referred to as "savages."

More recently, commercial anthropologists Patti Sunderland and Rita Denny (2007), conducted an ethnography for a beer company who wanted to know how university students decided what beers to order on a weekend night on the town. As was common, the client also wanted a video report they could see with their own eyes. Knowing that they would be a "fifth wheel" and would probably inhibit the students if they tagged along, the researchers enlisted one of the students to video record the group – something common in our video and selfie culture. What they found was that the students ordered "good" beers early in the evening when they could appreciate them and "cheap" beers later in the evening when they could not. This was not exactly an attempt to deeply understand weekend ritual drinking, but it was just what the client wanted. Unlike Malinowsky, in this case the ethnographers (or their surrogates) went to where the natives were rather than have the natives come to the researchers. And thanks to the short timeline of most commercial ethnography, the "anthropological year" also shrunk to a few weeks. The video form of their report is obviously something Malinowsky could not do either. But our ability to video record does not relieve the videographer from maintaining careful field notes. We have covered the basics of gathering video data in Chapter 6 and will examine doing video presentations in Chapter 10.

The advantage of including observation in ethnographic fieldwork, with or without photographs and video, is that it provides a view of what people actually do rather than what they say they do. Sometimes people do not realize that they do certain things or feel inhibited in describing them if they are intimate, sensitive, or socially taboo. If they don't realize they are doing something like furling their brow, they are unable to talk about it unless perhaps the researcher uses visual elicitation and show them a close-up of them doing so. At the same time, while observation can show us what people do, it can't show us why. Thus, neither observation nor interviews by themselves reveal the whole truth. But together they can come close and provide a more complete perspective. Interviews and video elicitation are more likely to provide an emic perspective on what certain actions, rituals, and behaviors mean to those engaging in them, whereas observation provides opportunities for capturing the unspoken details. Together, they give us the best of both worlds.

We have talked about some of the key data an ethnographic researcher gathers: interviews and transcripts (see Chapter 6), observations, fieldnotes, videos, photographs, and sound recordings. We should add to that artifacts and online material in the form of netnography. We will discuss netnography in the next section, but first consider the tangible artifacts that the researcher should gather.

Suppose we wish to understand a Midwestern American Independence Day celebration as we did in a project called the Consumer Behavior Odyssey (Belk, 1991; Belk, Wallendorf & Sherry, 1989). We couldn't cover everything or talk to everyone, but we were a diverse team and managed to examine a parade, a car show, a crafts show, a picnic, fireworks, and a few other venues in the small town where we spent the Fourth of July and the days surrounding it. Besides video, photos, and transcripts, we gathered local newspapers, parade programs, selected holiday souvenirs, and recordings of other local media coverage. We couldn't gather food artifacts, but we could taste them and record them in our reflexive journals of our fieldnotes. These were typically written at night as we perused the day's video recordings and artifacts. In those days we had to wait a day or two until our still photos were developed and printed, but those too prompted further recollections that we recorded in our typed fieldnotes. We had some of the first laptop computers, so at night and as we traveled, we sought to catch up on our field notes. This was also aided by listening to our audio recorders, into which we dictated spontaneous observations throughout the day as well as interviews we recorded. We were a group, but we did this independently and only later compared notes when we had finished our notes and transcriptions from a site. This was our attempt not to be influenced by the others' observations and insights until we got our own files done. But there is no hard and fast rule about this, and each ethnography develops its own procedures.

Different research projects require different approaches. The Fourth of July celebration described in the previous paragraph happens once a year, and fortunately we had a research team to try to capture it from multiple points of view. Arnould and Price (1993) studied commercial river rafting trips in the American West. While each trip took several days and involved a particular assemblage of people in multiple rafts, by taking many raft trips on multiple rivers they were able to get a more complete view of the phenomenon. They also literally exemplified the ethnographic adage that you can't step into the same river twice. That is, every experience, even in the same place with some of the same people, is unique. Even two members of the same trip, including the two ethnographers, will experience it differently. But group discussions help to highlight differences and similarities in perspectives and provide a more complete picture. Schau, Gilly and Wolfinbarger (2009) engaged in site-specific research by studying a retirement community. And Belk and Tumbat (2005) studied various fiercely loyal Apple consumers at a time when the company almost went bankrupt. As these examples show, the phenomenon of interest leads to different strategic approaches. Often the boundaries and time period for an ethnography cannot be fully specified ahead of time, and flexibility is a virtue.

Netnography

The ethnographic study of almost any phenomenon these days should begin with two procedures: a literature review and a netnography. The literature review, usually ranging over multiple academic disciplines, lets you learn what other related studies have found. You may want to overlap with prior research, but you will usually want to go further or explore a different angle. For instance, Diane Martin (Martin, Schouten & McAlexander, 2006) took a more female-focused perspective to better understand Harley Davidson motorcycle subculture that had been studied from a predominantly male point of view by Schouten and McAlexander (1995). The netnography imperative springs from a desire for a naturalistic point of view as found in the many social media and other online sites in which consumers come together virtually to discuss their interests and passions. Because they aren't participating in a study and are generally talking and posting to those who share their passion, netnographic material can be a great way to begin to learn about a phenomenon of interest.

Studying what people are saying online has a number of advantages as opposed to gathering more primary data from interviews and observation of behavior. These advantages include:

- More cost-effective
- Less work (automatically transcribed and logged)
- Less obtrusive (more natural)
- Less time-consuming (from your desk)
- Access to various groups around the world
- Can observe the past (archived threads)

- Large samples are possible
- Can access sensitive topics

For example, Belk (2022) used netnography to study owners of sex dolls. On several online sites, people posted posed photos of their sex dolls and told stories about them. Although it might be expected that all this content was pornographic and portrayed owners as macho men (and indeed some was), this was not the most common. Instead, the largely male owners of largely female sex dolls had to learn to care for the dolls, washing them, applying lotion, fixing their hair and make-up, shopping for clothes, and dressing them – all stereotypically feminine domains.

At the same time, there are also disadvantages and limitations compared to other methods:

- Cannot readily ascertain user demographics
- Loss of non-verbal information
- Loss of intangibles (e.g. silence, tone of voice)
- Integrity of information
- Information overload (too much of a good thing)
- Can't probe or ask questions

Some of these disadvantages and limitations can be overcome or compensated for by asking participants for interviews (with the permission of gatekeepers), reading emojis, emoticons, and other visuals, asking questions in online forums, and using multiple methods. It is also possible to use AI to summarize large amounts of content, but netnography is about small data sets in depth; it is not a Big Data method, although it may be used in combination with big data for a deeper understanding. As noted earlier, Kozinets (2023) has recently called for immersive netnography to study some online behavior, like that which takes place in fledgling metaverses. To do so it is necessary to construct a 3D avatar to interview others' 3D avatars in real time. One organization that facilitates creating your avatar is called "Ready Player Me" (after the metaverse book and movie "Ready Player One"). One of our authors, Russ Belk, had his avatar created by the company with the aid of a photo. A side-by-side comparison suggests at least a stylized resemblance (Figure 9.1):

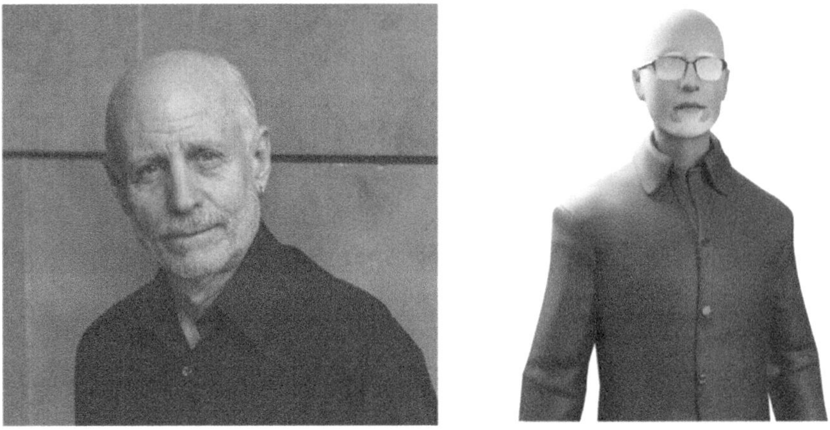

Figure 9.1 Author and avatar

As this attempt suggests, it is important to try to fit in the environment without looking farcical. While it might be disarming to have, say, a talking elephant avatar, chances are it wouldn't be taken seriously enough to get a good interview.

Step 1: Locate data

Robert Kozinets (2019) admits that some of his initial advice on doing netnography, like only studying existing online communities and always seeking web master permission (Kozinets, 2010), has fallen by the wayside. This is at least in part because the sorts of online material available have also changed, and methods need to change along with them. Moreover, the particular social media appropriate to your project depends on your focus:

> more than twice as many American women use Pinterest compared to men (41% versus 16%). Among young people aged 18–24, 78% use Snapchat (Smith & Anderson, 2018), versus only 7% among those aged 50 and over. And LinkedIn, which is a network for professionals, is somewhat unsurprisingly over five times more popular with high-income college graduates than those with a high school diploma or less (50% versus 9%). The median American social media user uses three social media platforms, and many Americans use several, with young adults showing the greatest variety of use.
>
> (Kozinets, 2019, p. 9)

These profiles continue to shift, and they also differ by location. For example, WeChat is dominant in China, while Reddit users are concentrated in the US (Figure 9.2):

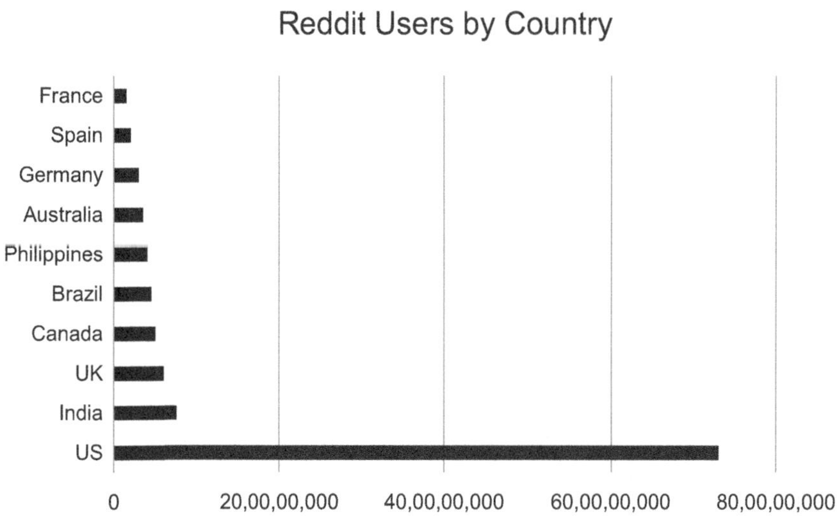

Figure 9.2 Reddit users

Source: Brian Dean (2024), "Reddit User and Growth Stats," Backlink, April 8, https://backlinko.com/reddit-users

And the greatest number of WhatsApp users are in India:

Table 9.1 WhatsApp users

Country	Number of Users
India	535.8 million
Brazil	168 million
Indonesia	112 million
United States	98 million
Philippines	88 million
Mexico	77 million
Russia	66.7 million
Turkey	60 million
Egypt	56 million
Pakistan	52 million

Source: Aarti Nair (2024), "WhatsApp Statistics for 2024 – All You Need to Know," *verloop.io*, April 13, https://verloop.io/blog/whatsapp-statistics-2024/#:~:text=1., surpass%203.14%20billion%20by%202025

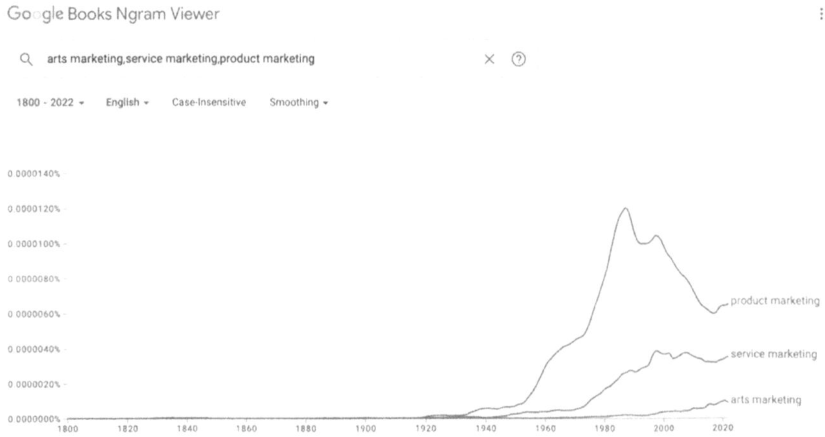

Figure 9.3 Ngram

So, the first step in conducting a netnography is to locate the best online sources of information. This depends not only on the location of users of a platform, but also on the topic, the amount of data available, and the nature of these data. For example, Instagram videos are short, whereas TikTok and YouTube may have short videos of varying lengths. Some are meant to entertain by creating and passing along memes and quips, while others are meant to inform and provide instruction. Some sites require subscriptions. Content is also subject to change, as are platform policies allowing or preventing researcher access.

While they are not a source of data for a netnography, you might begin to gain some context from "Big Data" sources like Google's Ngram viewer, which can show how frequently various topics show up in the content of books published in different periods of time (Figure 9.3).

A finer-grained look, but still not a qualitative netnographic source, is Google Trends. In Figure 9.2, we can compare the number of web searches for crypto, Ethereum, Bitcoin, and NFT (non-fungible token). It shows that there were spikes of apparent interest in all four terms during the 2020–2021 COVID-19 explosion of interest in crypto currencies like Bitcoin and the simultaneous bubble economy in NFTs and the Ethereum blockchain that underwrites most of them. The searches for these terms all peaked in 2021, when Christie's auction house sold Beeple's (Mike Winkleman's) collage of digital paintings called "Everydays: the First 5,000 Days" for $69.3 million. In early 2022, the bubble burst for NFTs and seemingly for Bitcoin and other cryptocurrencies. But despite losing two-thirds of its value in 2022, Bitcoin has come roaring back and by 2024 had regained its value and another 40% (Chandra & Belk, 2024).

But such data only suggest interesting questions that might be investigated using netnography. Why do people buy bitcoin? Why do they buy NFTs? Do NFTs represent a new art market? We can begin to address such questions in a netnography by examining what people say and have said over time about both types of speculative investments, a term that reflects their volatility (Humayun & Belk, 2022). All of this sets up the exercise that follows.

Exercise 9.1 Locating online material

For the problem just posed, locate promising online material by focusing on discussions of the pros and cons of "minting" (creating) or buying and selling NFTs today. Examine possible social media with these criteria in mind (Kozinets, 2019):

1. Relevance – matches what you are looking for
2. Activity – recency and frequency
3. Interactivity – not just one-way; ideally long strings of back-and-forth comments
4. Diversity – mixed voices
5. Richness – Deep ("thick" data)

We might add a sixth criterion of access. Seek open-access (public) sites.

Start a self-reflexive "immersion journal" about your experience locating these sites.

For a quick look at your data (or any other text, since this is an example), download any free word cloud programs. There is also an add-in for MS Word and PowerPoint, but you may not have access if you are using your institution's Office365. Try exploring how you can customize the display. Does it capture the essence of the data or text? Here is an example from a 9300-word paper by Sett and Belk:

Exercise 9.1

Step 2: Data analysis

Once you have located relevant online discussions, and in light of the amount of material available, you may need to narrow your focus, sample, truncate the period studied, or otherwise make the task of analyzing your data more manageable. The process of analyzing your data is similar to analyzing other ethnographic data. There are differences, however, that make it both easier and harder in the case of social media material. It may be easier because the data are already transcribed, because others interacting with writers (or other content-makers) may question or call out dubious posts and arguments, and because there is, at least ideally, a ready-made group of people interested in the same thing. But it is also harder because participants' demographic characteristics are generally unknown, the researcher usually can't probe and ask questions, the veracity of information cannot be assessed, and it may be hard to assess the roles and reputations of various participants. For example, it may take a while to learn who are the influencers and followers, the unspoken rules of the site, who is suspected of being a shill for a corporation, and who is always cynical, gullible, or knowledgeable and informative. Doubts about such things should be recorded in your immersive journal. Otherwise, the process of open, axial, and selective coding as well as abductive scrutiny should generally be followed (see Chapter 6).

The process of data analysis can be thought of as "pattern recognition." The researcher is looking for both similarities and differences from prior

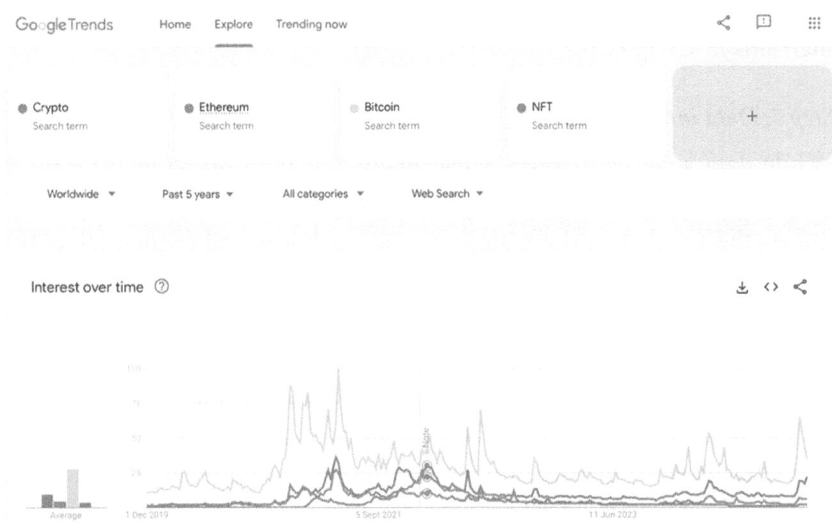

Figure 9.4 Google trends

findings, other parts of the data, other methods of data collection, or other online groups and sources. In part this is sense making, and in part it is triangulation to confirm or disrupt emerging interpretations. Kozinets (2019, p. 333) suggests using visualization methods including "tables, maps, charts, graphs, matrices, networks, and word clouds, data displays of various forms" to help in making sense of netnographic data. Like the data collection stage of netnography, researchers should include reflections on the analysis in the immersion journal (Figure 9.4).

In the word cloud example in Exercise 9.1, we found this to be a good reflection of the content, but we also would not have found it as helpful if we were not familiar with the data (paper in this case) that it was analyzing. This drives home the point that you must be intimately familiar with your data before attempting to make sense of it, especially with mechanical data reduction techniques like a word cloud. The same is true of using mechanical coding tools like those available in software programs like NVivo and ATLAS-ti. We will not discuss these programs here. It is not necessary to use them for analysis. We do not use them ourselves, and we feel that they create more distance between you and the data. On the other hand, we have seen others use them with great results. There is a bit more discussion of such aids in Chapter 6.

Step 3: Data interpretation

While data analysis involves sense-making, it does not constitute interpretation of your netnographic data. While the treatment here designates this as the third step, these steps are not as linear and sequential as this structure makes it appear. Interpretation usually begins in the field as you think about what you are hearing and seeing or accessing via other sensory modes. Even after you have all the data and some preliminary analyses completed, you may find reasons to go back to the original data and your archive of prior studies. This, in turn, may send you back to the library (or online equivalent) or back to your coding. In so doing you are "tacking." This is a sailing term derived from the way a sailboat can sail **into** the wind. It can't sail directly into the wind, so it zigzags a little to the left and then a little to the right until it reaches the sailor's objective. This is normal and a good thing. It may even send you back to the field to collect more data to check an emerging insight or a puzzle, surprise, or anomaly in the data (see Chapter 6 on abductive reasoning) in discussing it as a fourth coding stage. If the coding stage involves looking at fine details, interpretation is a stepping back and trying to gain a less detailed, more granular perspective on the data and coding. As Wolcott (1994) emphasizes, analysis transforms data, while interpretation transcends data. This means two things at once. First analysis is more about description, and interpretation is more about explanation; that is, analysis is more about what happened, and interpretation is more about why. Secondly, while analysis is very careful to be true to the data (and for this reason is often more emic), interpretation is more abstract and distant from the data (and for this reason is often more etic).

Interpretation is also more apt to use metaphors. Insights from projective data collection can be particularly relevant. Here is your chance to be creative and to search broadly for inspiration. Is there a song lyric that might apply? An ancient myth? A graphic novel? A movie plot (which may itself be inspired by one of the previous sources)? Deborah MacInnis (2011) suggests that first-year doctoral students are the most creative because they haven't yet had all the creativity beaten out of them by supervisors and faculty who tell them, "It wouldn't work," "It would take too long," "That will not look good on the job market," or "That doesn't address an existing conversation it the field." Actually, it starts earlier than that, when preschool teachers tell kids, "Color between the lines," "Grass is green, not gray," and "There is only one right answer." As Neal Postman (2018, p. 70) lamented, "Children enter school as question marks and leave as periods." But here's your chance to throw caution to the wind and think like a preschooler again. For example, in the manuscript from which the word cloud in Exercise 9.1 was created, we used conceptual artist Lawrence Weiner's observation (reported by Knight, 2007), that "Once you know about a work of mine you own it. There's no way I can climb inside your head and remove it" to offer an interpretation of NFTs, brand essence, music with an earworm, language, virtual reality, books, and the metaverse. It also resonates with some of the work by artists such as Yves Klein, Damian Hirst, Mauricio Cattelan, and Mike Winkleman.

Step 4: Publishing your netnography

Your netnography may or may not result in a standalone document worthy of publication by itself. It may be part of a larger project that could involve depth interviews (Chapter 6) and observation (see the next section). In this case, the netnography open up insights that can be probed with an interactive interview and tested against observations of actual behavior. Or it could be a follow-up study to a Big Data study of a larger data set relying on larger but thinner and decontextualized data sets. In this case, the smaller-scale deeper analysis of netnography is meant to drill down and provide a richer and culturally embedded understanding of a pattern identified in the Big Data study, which may well have been accompanied by AI-aided algorithmic inquiries.

In either of these cases, and sometimes with both combined, your task is to clarify your netnographic methods and detail how your findings help understand or contradict the prior Big Data insights and/or set up research questions to examine at the next stage of interviews and observations. How to communicate such findings effectively is a topic that is discussed in detail in Chapter 10.

Observation

Yogi Berra, famous New York Yankees baseball player and coach, was known for his insightful malapropisms and apparent tautologies. One example of such a quip is "You can observe a lot just by watching."There is some hidden truth here. Rather than passive looking and listening, we can learn much by careful observation and interpretation. We see with our eyes and hear with our ears, but we interpret with our mind. And this requires detailed attention to the behaviors, traces of behaviors, the context, and the culture in which the action takes place. Exercise 9.2 should provide you with an appreciation of this distinction as well as help develop your skills as an observer.

Exercise 9.2 A walk around the block

Take a walk around the block. It can be a familiar block or an unfamiliar block. You can adapt the instructions if you use a wheelchair, but go around the block in any case. Try to focus on your breathing, stride length, and the objective of getting some walking exercise. When you finish, write down everything you remember seeing, EVERYTHING. After this, go around the block again, paying attention to the homes, shops, and offices you see, even taking some smartphone photos or video recordings of things you find interesting about how people live, shop, and work (if people approach or question you, explain your project and ask their permission). Now write up your observations and reflections on the insights you have about the neighborhood. Compare this understanding to your more casual initial account. One final variant is to walk around the block in reverse and test your insights.

Autoethnography

Observation can be participant observation or non-participant observation. An additional format is self-observation or *auto-ethnography*, in which case the self-reflexive and possibly introspective aspects of observation take center stage (e.g., Kapoor, Patterson & O'Malley, 2020; Zouaoui, 2024). The autoethnography can also look backward in time because you were there. This is a bit like extracting an *Oral History* of another person, which might be considered a guided elicitation, perhaps aided by the objects in the person's home if that is where the oral history is being gathered (see Kapoor & Belk, 2022).

Autoethnography and oral history can take courage, as the passage in Textbox 9.1 illustrates.

> ***Textbox 9.1 Excerpt from an autoethnography***
>
> Looking back on my childhood years, I would say that I was happily dumb. I wasn't aware that my body shape, or the fact that I was a chubby or fat kid, would mean so much to the world or society. My body acted as a moral/social signifier that became the major criterion to classify me as 'in' or 'out' most of the time (Belk, 2019). It was, and still is, the only real home my soul ever truly enjoyed. God knows this isn't easy when your inside doesn't match your outside most of the time. In my circle of friends (sisters, girls, guys), I am always the youngest, weirdest, and fattest. That makes me very noticeable, even though most of the time I don't really seek the spotlight and am much more comfortable in the shadows, as I learned to be. However, living in such a body makes it evident that I will likely the first thing that catches the eye: 'the giant elephant in the room,' as some would say (Zouaoui, 2024, p. 222).

Mechanical observation

By observation, we mean primarily by human observers. There are, however, enough CCTV cameras around the world that in certain cases we might benefit from checking their surveillance footage in real time and sometimes retroactively. There are many sites that provide access to such video material. Search for "live CCTV footage" and you will probably find some. For example, if this link to the Elbo Room bar in Fort Lauderdale, Florida is still active, you (https://www.youtube.com/watch?v=KY4Yd5QR570) might observe for five minutes and see how you would describe what is going on. If not, try to find another live bar scene elsewhere and do the same. You might even compare such a bar in the American southeast to one in, say, Finland. Streaming such video content online raises ethical questions of consent (usually, there must be a sign warning participants of this possibility), but public and commercial surveillance records are widely available online.

If you have access to mechanically gathered video, there is a question of what to look for or listen for. For example, try the observation tasks in Exercise 9.3.

Exercise 9.3 Guided and unguided observation

- First, watch the four minutes of video at https://www.youtube.com/watch?v=Y-s0pIHTac4.
- Now, where was this? What brands did you see? What kinds of vehicles? What was the most common vehicle color? What time of day was it? What time of year? What were people doing besides walking? How could you tell?
- Now try watching again with these questions in mind. How much difference did it make? This is the difference between unguided and guided observation.

There are also trade-offs between structured and unstructured observation, as this video using a structured procedure shows: https://www.youtube.com/watch?v=VgTpAoJEXaE. Like the monkey business illusion (https://www.youtube.com/watch?v=IGQmdoK_ZfY), when you are looking for one thing you may do a good job of spotting it, but you may miss other things going on around you.

Non-participant and unobtrusive observation

The mechanical observations discussed in the previous section, with the exceptions of autoethnography and oral history, are all non-participant observation methods. But there are others. It is useful to note that there are many aspects of art and art design consumption that are inherently visual. This includes the design of art and culture museums and exhibitions, artworks themselves, design and management of online representations by art and culture institutions, visual historic research, and the 3D multiverse. For instance, you could look, albeit possibly in vain (Chandra & Belk, 2024), for visual features that predict the value of NFTs of a certain sort, like bored apes from the Bored Ape Yacht Club collection.

One set of techniques called unobtrusive methods were described by Webb et al. (1966, 1999). The book was initially entitled *The Bullfighter's Beard*, because it was observed that facial hair on males grows faster if the person is anxious. They found that this folk wisdom tended to predict how likely the matador was to be gored by the bull in a bullfight. The point of unobtrusive measures is that they are records of naturalistic behaviors that do not involve asking questions or being a known participant observer, both of which might cause people to behave unnaturally. One unobtrusive measure that we have already considered and discussed in the netnography section is archival data. Besides extensively analyzing a group of posts to a social media site, we might also use the posts, photos, and videos of participants (with their permission and possible collaboration) for video or other presentation (see Chapter 10). This is something that Cavusoglu and Belk (2024) did for a project on facial differences discussed in Chapter 6.

Other types of unobtrusive measures include accretion, physical trace, simple observation, and contrived observation. The Chicago Museum of Science and Industry wanted to learn which of its exhibits were more popular. They could have stationed an interviewer at the exit and asked people, but they feared this could result in a bias in favor of socially desirable answers (e.g., the history of education exhibit over the history of contraception exhibit). So they pulled up the floor tiles in front of each exhibit and put down new floor tiles. They then pulled up the floor tiles and measured wear as an index of popularity. This is an accretion measure – how much something builds up or wears down. Can you see any potential problems with this method that could lead to spurious results? They needed to consider the location of the exhibits and exclude those on the way to the cafeteria, gift shop, or toilets.

Another unobtrusive method is physical trace measures. These are things TV detectives look for as clues to who-done-it – footprints, fingerprints, DNA, and so forth. In the case of arts research, we could also use some careful sleuthing. The height of nose prints on a display window might give an indication of the age of children showing an interest in what is behind the glass. There is even a field called "garbology" that looks at trash collected from various neighborhoods to see what certain areas eat, drink, read (at least in print media), and dispose of (Rathje & Murphy, 1992). This can inform us about health information, diets, and interests. The most popular American sports event is the Superbowl. The change in water pressure at a certain time on Superbowl Sunday in various cities is a good instant measure of audience size at that locale. The time is the start of halftime, because this is when those who had been glued to their TVs or other devices all decide to go to the toilet and flush it after use. If some cities did not adjust the water supply accordingly, it could break the system.

Simple and contrived observation are unobtrusive measures that are basically what they sound like. The URLs people search for on computer demos give evidence of what sorts of price comparisons they might be searching for. This is a simple unobtrusive observation. A contrived observation arranges a situation – how much do various types of signs (e.g., "Please" versus "don't") do to reduce litter? Does a fake stalled car at an intersection prompt more honks if it is a high-status or low-status car? A Tesla electric vehicle or a big-engine "muscle car"?

These are just a few examples of unobtrusive measures. Use your imagination to think of others in your area of research interest. When the researcher is ostensibly more obtrusive, such measures are non-participant or simple observation. Weighing the food on the plates of children in a school cafeteria, and perhaps relating it to gender, age, and the child's weight is an example.

Conclusion

The observational, netnographic, and ethnographic methods discussed in this chapter are a valuable complement to depth interviews. What people say they do is, for various reasons, not what people actually do. They may forget, be unaware, by constrained by socially desirable self-presentation, or be otherwise inhibited or given to exaggeration or minimization. Because some of this data (e.g., netnographic, unobtrusive) is free for the taking, we might assume it is a part of every research report on human behavior. Unfortunately, it is not. Despite the problems just noted, we continue to put too much faith in what people say they do.

References

Angrosino, M. (2007), *Doing ethnographic observational research*. Los Angeles: Sage.

Arnould, E. & Price, L. (1993), "River magic: Extraordinary experience and the extended service encounter," *Journal of Consumer Research*, 20(1), 24–45.

Belk, R. (Ed.). (1991), *Highways and buyways: Naturalistic research from the consumer behavior Odyssey*. Provo, UT: Association for Consumer Research.

Belk, R. (2019), "On Standing Out and Fitting in," *Journal of Global Fashion Marketing*, 10(3), 203–227.

Belk, R. (2022), "Artificial emotions and love and sex doll service workers," *Journal of Service Research*, 25(4), 521–536.

Belk, R., Fischer, E., & Kozinets, R. (2013), *Qualitative consumer and marketing research*. Los Angeles: Sage.

Belk, R., & Kozinets, R. (2024), "Videographic and visual consumer research: The state of the art," in F. Kawaf (Ed.), *Visual methods in marketing and consumer research* (pp. 35–55). London: Routledge.

Belk, R., & Tumbat, G. (2005), "The cult of Macintosh," *Consumption, Markets and Culture*, 8(3), 205–217.
Belk, R., Wallendorf, M., & Sherry, J. (1989), "The sacred and the profane in consumer behavior: Theodicy on the Odyssey," *Journal of Consumer Research*, 15(1), 1–38.
Boellstorff, T. (2008), *Coming of age in second life: An anthropologist explores the virtually human*. Princeton, NJ: Princeton University Press.
Cavusoglu, L., & Belk, R. (2024), "How to make a collaborative videography using phygital affordances to study sensitive topics," *Qualitative Market Research*, 27(3), 413–432.
Chandra, Y., & Belk, R. (2024), "Is that JPEG worth 70 million dollars? Value creation and perceptions of non-fungible tokens in a bubble economy," *Journal of Marketing Management*. https://www.tandfonline.com/doi/abs/10.1080/0267257X.2024.2425691.
Hackley, C. (2020), *Qualitative research in marketing and management: Doing interpretive research projects*. London: Routledge.
Heath, C., Hindmarsh, J., & Luff, P. (2010), *Video in qualitative research: Analyzing social interaction in everyday life*. Los Angeles, CA: Sage.
Heisley, D., & Levy, S. (1991), "Autodriving: A photoelicitation technique," *Journal of Consumer Research*, 18(3), 257–282.
Humayun, M., & Belk, R. (2022), "How brand hive minds thrive: Understanding bitcoin's resilience," *Cryptoeconomic Systems*, 2(1). https://cryptoeconomicsystems.pubpub.org/pub/humayun-bitcoin-brandresilience/release/2?readingCollection=082fed82.
Kapoor, V. M., & Belk, R. (2022), "Coping and career choices: Irish gay men's passage from hopelessness to redemption," *Consumption Markets & Culture*, 25(1), 52–78.
Kapoor, V. M., Patterson, M., & O'Malley, L. (2020), "Liminal consumption of 'the cosmic ballet': An autoethnography," *Consumption Markets & Culture*, 23(1), 61–80.
Knight, N. (2007), "Slowly adapting art: Moving with the times: Re-installing original." https://www2.oberlin.edu/stupub/ocreview/2007/04/27/arts/Slowly_Adapting_Art_Moving.html.
Kozinets, R. (2010), *Netnography: Doing ethnographic research online*. London: Sage.
Kozinets, R. (2019), *Netnography: The essential guide to qualitative social media research* (3rd ed.). Los Angeles: Sage.
Kozinets, R. (2023), "Immersive netnography: A novel method for service experience research in virtual reality, augmented reality and metaverse contexts," *Journal of Service Management*, 34(1), 100–125.
MacInnis, D. (2011), "A framework for conceptual contributions in marketing," *Journal of Marketing*, 75(4), 84–102.
Malinowski, B. (1922), *Argonauts of the Western Pacific*. London: Routledge and Kegan Paul.
Malinowski, B. (1926), *Crime and custom in a savage society*. London: Routledge and Kegan Paul.
Martin, D., Schouten, J., & McAlexander, J. (2006), "Claiming the throttle: Multiple femininities in a hyper-masculine subculture," *Consumption, Markets and Culture*, 9(3), 171–205.
Moisander, J., & Valtonen, A. (2006), *Qualitative marketing research: A cultural approach*. London: Sage.
Pink, S. (2001), *Doing visual ethnography*. London: Sage.
Postman, N. (2018), *The end of education: Redefining the value of school*. New York: Knopf.
Rathje, W., & Murphy, C. (1992), *Rubbish! The archaeology of garbage: What our garbage tells us about ourselves*. New York: HarperPerennial.
Schau, H., Gilly, M., & Wolfinbarger, M. (2009), "Consumer identity renaissance: The resurgence of identity-inspired consumption in retirement," *Journal of Consumer Research*, 36(2), 255–276.
Schouten, J., & McAlexander, J. (1995), "Subcultures of consumption: An ethnography of the new bikers," *Journal of Consumer Research*, 22(1), 43–62.

Smith, A., & Anderson, M. (2018), "Social media use in 2018," Washington, DC: Pew Internet & American Life Project. www.pewinternet.org/2018/03/01/social-media-use-in-2018/.

Sunderland, P. & Denny, R. (2007), *Doing Antpphropology in Consumer Research*, London: Routledge.

Tian, K., & Belk, R. (2005), "Extended self and possessions in the workplace," *Journal of Consumer Research*, 32(2), 297–310.

Webb, E., Campbell, D., Schwartz, R., & Sechrest, L. (1966), *Unobtrusive measures: Nonreactive research in the social sciences*. Chicago: Rand McNalley.

Webb, E., Campbell, D., Schwartz, R., & Sechrest, L. (1999), *Unobtrusive measures* (Revised ed.). Chicago: Rand McNalley.

Wolcott, H. (1994), *Transforming qualitative data*. Thousand Oaks, CA: Sage.

Zouaoui, H. (2024), "Autoethnography: Steering away from too much about introspection," in R. Belk, & C. Otnes (Eds.), *Handbook of qualitative research methods in marketing* (2nd ed., pp. 221–231). Cheltenham, UK: Edward Elgar.

10

Effective writing and presentations

Introduction

In academic research we want to share our discoveries with the world, or at least with other academics. In more proprietary research we at least want to convince a corporate managerial audience of our insights and their implications. This is true whether we are presenting the implications to a for-profit or non-profit corporate board. In each case we want to present fresh insights and advocate for certain actions based on our findings that are clearly and engagingly presented. As with data collection and analysis methods, we should consider a wide variety of output media possibilities, from PowerPoint and Canva slide decks to journal articles, films, online media, and chapters or books. The presentations may be live, archived, broadcast, or involve transmedia storytelling. But regardless of the medium, all writing and presentations invite storytelling. Because we are doing research by gathering evidence of something, our stories must be, at least in some sense, true. But that doesn't mean they are dry "just the facts" recitations. They are ideally designed to convey insights, to make sense of things, to move the audience to experience an emotion, or to make us feel what it is like to be another person or to have a particular experience. In this chapter, we cover both written and audio-visual presentations in the form of films and broadcast or narrowcast videos.

DOI: 10.4324/9781003487951-10

Step 1: Preparing to communicate your research

Perhaps the biggest mistake that new researchers make at this stage of the process is to start writing a draft or scripting an audio-visual presentation without planning out the story that they want to tell. Good writing incorporates three distinct phases: outlining, drafting, and revising. While it is tempting to skip the outlining step and move straight to drafting, that is likely to lead to a draft that is poorly organized and difficult for the reader to follow. This, in turn, will require many more revisions and is more likely to be rejected if submitted for publication. The quality of your research presentation is strongly correlated with the quality of your outlining and planning.

There are two forms of outlines that can be helpful in planning to communicate academic research. The first is an outline of the literature. Presumably, when you were conducting your literature review as discussed in Chapter 4, you took notes on what you were reading. This could be in a Word document, an Excel spreadsheet, or using a reference software package. While it is important and valuable to take notes on each individual source, before beginning the writing process it is helpful to revisit these notes and integrate them into an outline of the literature stream as a whole. One possible approach is to develop a timeline of the literature in chronological order, from the oldest or most seminal works to the most recent. This should not be a complete rewriting of your notes on each paper. Rather, try to consolidate the main points of each paper into one or two sentences. If there is a particular reason you plan to cite a specific paper, for example, for the definition of a core construct or the source of a particular measure, note that in the outline. As an alternative, you might use a visual presentation such as a literature map, with each source represented as a node, and sources that build on each other or are theoretically connect linked together, either in a network or hierarchically.

The second is an outline of the story that you wish to tell, the narrative of the paper or presentation without the details or citations incorporated at this stage. For example, you might develop an "elevator pitch" for your research, imagining how you might explain it to someone you are chatting with for a few minutes. You might alternatively draft a "paper in a page," a one-page summary that tells the story of your paper in narrative form, similar to an extended abstract. You might also find it helpful to construct an outline patterned on the structure of a mathematical proof, beginning with a statement that your reader would agree with and listing the steps that flow logically from that statement to your proposed contribution. This narrative outline can then be combined with your literature outline, indicating which sources you intend to cite to support each element of your narrative, thus creating a complete outline of the draft that you plan to write.

Although the process of planning and editing a film is different from that of writing an article, chapter, or book, in each case there is a pre- and/or post-summary of what your study has discovered. Thus, an important starting point is to write a one-paragraph summary. This paragraph may be modified and refined as your presentation evolves, but writing out a tentative summary is nevertheless an important first step, even before you attempt a more detailed outline or storyboard. This sounds easy, but it is surprisingly challenging. The paragraph should ideally convey the following:

1. What is the phenomenon or concept you are studying?
2. What is your research question?
3. What methods and research paradigm did you use?
4. What did you find?
5. Why is that important and interesting?
6. What are the implications of what you have found?

This paragraph, or video trailer in the case of a video, should pique the reader's/viewer's interest and invite and excite them to "read" on. Use short and jargon-free well-written sentences that grip the reader or viewer in an engaging mystery.

In the case of a video, incorporate compelling images and sounds as well. Watch some previews and trailers for feature films, documentaries, and television series. Don't be afraid to use background music generated by AI to generate excitement and an appropriate mood. For example, in the film for the collaborative participatory action research project on people with severe facial differences by Cavusoglu and Belk (2023a, 2023b; see also Chapter 6), we created a trailer composed of 45 seconds of video with music and lower-thirds titles (Cavusoglu & Belk, 2023b). In the main video, we avoided "voice of God" narration in favor of letting participants speak for themselves. In order to set expectations, however, we present some brief summary statistics in the trailer (e.g., 1 in 10 people have a facial difference). Together, the trailer and video make a compelling case against the medical and ableist belief that those with facial differences have a problem that needs to be "fixed" with medical intervention.

Step 2: Framing the phenomenon and research question

Academic writing is, at its core, persuasive writing. The first step in persuading your audience that your research is interesting is to hook them with a compelling illustration of the phenomenon you wish to study that sets up your research question. In rhetoric, this approach is referred to as *pathos*, persuading through evoking an emotional response in your audience.

In the project on facial differences, we used the interviews along with the video shots we requested of participants getting ready in the morning to show the phenomenon. Interview clips and participants' videos and still photos going back to childhood for those with congenital differences are also used to describe the bullying, name-calling, stares, and fright that those with differences in appearance face. We let the participants tell their stories without our comments, except for the headings that we used to organize the film after some of our key participants introduce themselves and their stories:

1. Facing Society
2. Facing Media
3. Facing Self
4. Facing Stigma
5. Facing Prejudice
6. Facing ME

Since the topic is "heavy," we also use humor to lighten the mood, as when Duane shows and talks about taking his artificial ears off before going to bed and refers to himself as "Mr. Potato-head." Later in the film, Ladarius describes such self-deprecating practices as a negative coping mechanism, offering an alternative point of view. We also use music to soften or heighten audience emotions as our participants describe their experiences in each of the six organizing categories enumerated here. We use subtitles for foreign languages used by participants from Brazil, Turkey, and India. But we avoid offering our own interpretations.

Besides the video, we also have several written papers that have their own techniques of introducing the focal phenomenon. For example, for one written paper currently under review, we use an excerpt from Nathanael West's (1933) novel, *Miss Lonelyhearts*, to introduce our research on people with severe facial differences:

Dear Miss Lonelyhearts –

I am sixteen years old now and I dont know what to do and would appreciate it if you could tell me what to do. When I was a little girl it was not so bad because I got used to the kids on the block making fun of me, but now I would like to have boy friends like the other girls and go out on Saturday nites, but no boy will take me because I was born without a nose – although I am a good dancer and have a nice shape and my father buys me pretty clothes.

I sit and look at myself all day and cry. I have a big hole in the middle of my face that scares people even myself so I cant blame the boys for not wanting to take me out. My mother loves me, but she crys terrible when she looks at me.

What did I do to deserve such a terrible bad fate? Even if I did do some bad things I didnt do any before I was a year old and I was born this way. I asked Papa and he says he doesnt know, but that maybe I did something in the other world before I was born or that maybe I was being punished for his sins. I dont believe that because he is a very nice man. Ought I commit suicide?

Sincerely yours,

Desperate (West, 1933, p. 5)

The novel is considered an American classic and a satiric take on a newspaper advice columnist who is overwhelmed with letters from the grieving. They pray to him for help, and all he can offer are platitudes. But the excerpt from the novel is used in our paper (Cavusoglu & Belk, 2023a, 2023b) to foreshadow the dilemmas of those we studied. It implicitly poses our research question: What are the dilemmas that those with facial differences must deal with, and how do they cope with or triumph over these dreadful adversities? It will be noted that the "what" and "how" here are descriptive research questions. Like the video (Cavusoglu & Belk, 2023a, 2023b), the research is part of a collaborative participatory action research (PAR) project, and it is intended to advocate for anti-ableist action to create acceptance like that recently achieved by the LGBTQ+ community. The underlying theoretical framework involves coping strategies and ableism. Thus, there are theoretical contributions in the study, but they are not the main focus. We disclose our advocacy objective early in the paper.

While not all research topics lend themselves to this depth of illustration, think about how you can create an image or understanding of the importance of your phenomenon in the minds of your audience members. If you can get your audience to care about your phenomenon, they are more likely to see your research question, and therefore your research, as interesting and valuable.

Once you have illustrated the importance of your phenomenon and established your research question, make sure that you are also clearly stating the contribution that your research intends to make. Recall from Chapter 2 that there are a variety of ways to make a contribution with your research. For academic journal articles in particular, it is essential for your introduction to clearly state what your contribution is and to which literature stream you are contributing. This is again a question of audience. Remember the questions we asked in Chapter 2 when developing a research question:

1. Who am I talking to?
2. What are they talking about?
3. What am I adding to the conversation?
4. Why should they care about what I am saying?

These same questions should be evident in your introduction as part of establishing your phenomenon of interest and research question. In particular, you need to present a compelling answer to the fourth question for your reader to find your research question important and valuable. "This has not previously been studied" is not a sufficient argument for your audience. "This needs to be studied because . . ." is a much more compelling argument.

Step 3: Writing a literature review and theoretical foundation

Once you have established a compelling phenomenon and created an emotional response in your audience, you now need to build a persuasive argument for your contribution using the rhetorical tools of *ethos*, establishing your credibility, and *logos*, persuading through logic.

One potential source of *ethos* or credibility is your literature review. By grounding your argument in literature, you establish credible support for your conclusions as well as demonstrating your scholarship and understanding of the knowledge in the field. This should not be a replication of your literature outline or otherwise systematic listing of sources on the topic, and it should not be separated from your theoretical foundation or hypothesis development, if included. You will want to avoid the simple realist approach of saying A said X, B said Y, and C said Z, or worse yet a table of prior related articles with basic parameters like methods, findings, and dates. This spreadsheet approach is like the reductionism of SLRs (Systematic Literature Reviews). Nor should the literature review be used merely for carving out a space for the present study (i.e., the phenomenon has not been studied before, therefore this study fills that gap). This is like the businessman that the Little Prince found on the fourth planet he visited. The man was busy tallying up the stars that he insisted he owned: "When you're the first person to have an idea, you patent it and it's yours. Now I own the stars since no one before me has ever thought of owning them" (Saint-Exupéry, 1943/2000, p. 39). Rather, there should be a narrative that weaves the literature into a coherent narrative, including the writer's evaluations and interpretations of the research. This also provides the opportunity to position the present research within this interpretive narrative. The literature review should also be broad and cover work in other disciplines and journals if it is relevant. Exercise 10.1 will help you to analyze literature reviews based on this criterion.

Exercise 10.1

Choose two or three articles on topics germane to your research interests. First, examine the literature review and see how it does on the previous recommendations (impressionism, coherent narrative, evaluation, and breadth). Second, look at the writing style of the paper. Is it interesting? Non-formulaic? Largely devoid of jargon? Third, look at the citation count of the paper in Google Scholar. Is the average number of citations per year related to any of these characteristics?

We saw in step 2 that fiction can be part of the introduction by artistically presenting a compelling phenomenon. Photos can help do this as well. Unlike the anonymity of quantitative research, in qualitative storytelling we may sometimes use images of our participants, with their permission and signed consent forms. This is something Cavusoglu and Belk (2024) did in a methods paper on Collaborative Videography. Pink (2001) suggests that photographs and writing in the present tense add a sense of authority and authenticity to the narrative. But Van Maanen (1988, p. 11) warns that gratuitous photos in ethnographies merely attest to the writer's presence. However, he notes that photos can also be used because they are evocative. This was the intent in our study of facial differences. Rather than the self-affirming presence of the ethnographer in what Van Maanen (1988) calls the dispassionate third person "realist" tale, stories and images that evoke emotions are better grouped in the category he calls "impressionist" tales, drawing from the art movement of the late nineteenth- and early twentieth-century painters like Renoir, Van Gogh, Seurat, and Monet. Impressionist tales leave something to the imagination. As Chatman (1978, p. 29) observes,

> A Dutch still life painter may include an exact reproduction of minutiae in the set-up before him [sic], down to the smallest dewdrop on a peach, while the Impressionist may dash off a distant pedestrian with a single brush stroke.

The second source of *ethos* or credibility is your empirical findings, discussed in the next section. While a quantitative research paper that develops hypotheses should support theoretical conclusions prior to presenting the methodology and findings, a qualitative research paper can integrate the literature review with the interpretation of the empirical findings and/or support theoretical arguments with empirical data from the study.

This is where the final step of persuasive writing, *logos* or logic, comes into play. Regardless of your research goal or methodological approach, if your findings can be completely explained by existing literature, then you have not made a contribution. Thus, there should be a point where grounding in the literature is no longer possible and your theoretical argument, whether part of hypothesis development or interpretation of qualitative findings, must go beyond what we already know and rely on a logical extension of existing knowledge. This is where you are developing theory.

It can help to get a friendly review and editorial help if you are writing in your second language. Be sure to cite anything relevant that has been published in the target journal, whether you present it favorably or not. The journal wants to increase its impact factor with many citations. Besides writing in the format of the journal submission guidelines, read extensively in the journal's published papers to determine its unwritten writing conventions. Remember to break up long sentences into multiple shorter sentences and to avoid jargon whenever possible. Ideally, people from multiple disciplines will discover your paper, and you want to avoid unnecessary barriers to understanding.

Step 4: Writing methods sections and findings

The methods section is where you have the opportunity to describe and explain to your reader exactly what you did to collect and analyze your data. Methods which may be inventive can nonetheless be rendered in a straightforward way. Every methodological approach has a standard for how it is described and what information must be reported. It is a good idea to consult several recent examples of papers using your methodology published in your target journal and model your methods section on what they report.

Once you have described your methods, it is time to report your findings. Again, there are standards associated with each different methodology for how findings should be reported. For quantitative research, this section reports and interprets the results of statistical analyses that test the hypotheses along with any appropriate preliminary or post hoc tests. For qualitative research, this is where the data is interpreted and the themes explicated to connect to the theoretical findings and research question. This section may also address the context if it is likely to be unfamiliar to most readers. But ultimately, it is the *concepts* that emerge from the analysis and findings that are important – not the *context* (Askegaard & Linnet, 2011; Price, Moisio & Arnould, 2024).

Depending on your research method and research goal, either the theoretical foundation section or the findings section may conclude with a visual model or diagram. If your research goal is to explain, predict, or test causes, then a "boxes and arrows" conceptual model of predictive or causal relationships is most appropriate and would likely be placed at the end of the theoretical foundation section, before the methods section. If your research goal is to describe or understand, then this type of conceptual model would not be appropriate, but a model or diagram that in some way illustrates the relationships between the concepts or themes in your findings is still highly valuable. This is your chance to be creative and to make your findings come alive for readers. After the title and abstract, many readers look only for a diagram that summarizes your findings. Play with graphics, perhaps using the free version of Crave plus the optional features of Word and PowerPoint. Like selective coding and abductive techniques (see Chapter 6), these should be a step removed from the data and both your most abstract and important findings, not little details that detract from the main theoretical contribution. Exercise 10.2 will help you to examine the breadth of options available for visually depicting your findings or theoretical ideas.

Exercise 10.2

Look at recent journals in your area of interest to find good and bad examples of illustrative figures. If you have some research findings, try to develop a diagram that you believe is clear and illustrates your key finding(s). It should stand on its own. If you do not have findings, try illustrating a conceptual model in your area of interest. Finally, ask a colleague if your illustration is clear to them and how they would interpret it.

Besides any diagrams and the abstract (best written last for consistency with findings and major contributions), the findings themselves are the key consideration in the review process and for those readers who actually go through the paper in detail. As with the literature review, this is a narrative that should be well-crafted. Write, rewrite, revise, and repeat until you are happy with the result.

Step 5: Writing discussion and conclusion sections

If the introduction is your opportunity to hook the reader with an interesting phenomenon and important research question, then the discussion and conclusion is your opportunity to persuade the reader of the value and relevance of your ideas and conclusions. This section often begins with a brief summary of your findings, but that should not be the main focus of the discussion section. This section is the "so what" of your findings – a discussion of how what you have found should change the way researchers think about their future research and/or how managers should change the way they think about their future practical decisions.

For example, a theoretical contribution might follow one of these general forms:

- Previously, we assumed that this phenomenon only occurred under X conditions. However, I have shown that this phenomenon extends to Y conditions. This means that moving forward, researchers will need to think about Y conditions as well as X conditions when theorizing about this phenomenon.
- Previously, we assumed that this phenomenon occurred under all conditions related to X. However, I have shown then when Y conditions occur, this phenomenon no longer holds/changes direction/is stronger/weaker. This means that moving forward, researchers will need to consider how Y conditions affect this phenomenon and/or consider other conditions that may change the direction/strength of the phenomenon.
- Previously, we assumed that participants experienced this phenomenon as X. However, I have shown that their own perspectives on the phenomenon are more closely related to Y. This means that moving forward, researchers should be thinking about this phenomenon from the perspective of Y, and not the perspective of X.

While a methodological contribution might follow a form like this:

- Previously, we assumed that the best way to measure/proxy/capture this phenomenon was using X. However, I have shown that Y does a better job of measuring/proxying/capturing the phenomenon. This means that moving forward, researchers should use my measure/proxy/method when they are studying the phenomenon.

Managerial implications should follow theoretical or methodological implications in the discussion section only when they are appropriate. A desire to find managerial implications in every study of some type of managerial implications can lead to statements like, "We found that consumers with this personality trait are more likely to engage in this behavior, so organizations who are trying to accomplish this goal should target consumers with this personality trait." Organizations do not give their consumers personality tests! To write good managerial implications, start by thinking about a specific managerial audience. Do you have recommendations for organizations, for specific decision-makers within organizations, for government or public policy makers, or for consumers, employees, investors, or other stakeholders of the organization? Think about what actions these audiences realistically have available to them. Generic recommendations like "organizations should build stronger brand communities" are not actionable implications. Think about where consumers interact with the organization, what tools the organization has available to them, and how they might use those tools to accomplish the positive outcomes or avoid the negative consequences that you identified through your research findings.

Finally, every research design necessarily has limitations that should be acknowledged as part of the discussion section. A typical limitations section relies on generic, mostly unactionable limitations that are common to all research; for example, "the data was gathered cross-sectionally and we should study the phenomenon longitudinally," or "the data was gathered within one specific context, and we should study the phenomenon across cultures/industries." Rather than relying on these platitudes, think critically about your own research design and findings and how you can expand on it. What would you have done differently in a perfect world? What findings surprised you, and how would you change things now that you know them? How can you expand on what you have done to gain a deeper understanding of the phenomenon you have uncovered? Where do you go from here?

Writing for a managerial audience

There are differences in presentation to managerial audiences versus academic audiences. Topics such as branding, advertising, store design and layout, social media, customer service, and museum patronage are likely to interest both business and academia (Akaka & Schau, 2024; Denny, 2024; Denny & Sunderland, 2014; Joy & Sherry, 2003; Östberg & Hartman, 2024). Practical or managerial implications are expected, but businesses are also interested in conceptual papers and studies of emerging phenomena like the Metaverse (e.g., Belk, Humayun & Brouard, 2022; Yang & Chattopadhyay, 2024).

Discussion and conclusion sections of a research publication will also differ depending on whether managers, politicians, or academics are the primary expected audience. Emphasis on practical versus theoretical is one major difference. Belk, Fischer and Kozinets (2013, pp. 177–180) offer the following suggestions for presenting qualitative research to a managerial audience:

1. **Contextualize the data** – e.g., is care of pets about foods, medicines, toys, or services?
2. **Analyze figures of speech such as tropes and metaphors** – e.g., how do consumers understand "homemade"?
3. **Attend to contradictions in the data** – e.g., cultural differences in color symbolism.
4. **Reveal moments of revelation** – e.g., frustrations with paper napkins (serviettes) in eating certain foods such as tacos.
5. **Explore discontinuities between talk and action** – e.g., those who say they "eat healthy" but who have cupboards full of potato chips (crisps), cookies (biscuits), and candies (lollies).
6. **Maintain some productive contact with academic theory** – e.g., ethnic food cultures and cultural theory.

When academics write for other academics, they more or less share the same professional culture. This is not necessarily the case when they write for marketing managers. Although they may share an interest in some of the same topics, like brands, events, and advertising, their focus, vocabulary, and time frame may well differ. Some appreciation of such differences is helpful.

Conclusion

The steps recommended in this chapter are just suggestions. You should feel free to experiment and use whatever methods work for you. Be creative. Polish by rewriting and bringing in whatever is relevant from your reading and background. Be aware of the conventions and style sheets of the journal for which you are writing. Chances are you will have too many words rather than too few, based on journal page or word limits. Cutting huge amounts of text forces you to decide what really matters. Put some effort (and perhaps AI) into creating the perfect succinct figure that summarizes your contribution. Use other relevant illustrations and graphics as well. There may be exceptions, like our facial difference project, but normally disguise your participants and follow your informed consent protocol promises.

Know your audience and write for them. Pick the most appropriate journal for your paper, but always err on the side of choosing the more highly rated journal. Revise when given the opportunity, and address the reviewer comments highlighted by the editor or associate editor (AE). Push back when you feel advice is inappropriate or the reviewers have missed something. But don't be argumentative just because you don't like the advice. Give yourself a few days to cool off if necessary.

If your paper is rejected or desk-rejected, learn from it. Fix the problems highlighted before sending it to another journal. Chances are that one or more of the reviewers from journal A will also be a reviewer for journal B, so never send off the same exact paper rejected by journal A to journal B.

Finally, find joy in writing well, being creative, and developing good conceptual models that can be shown visually. All of this begins by choosing an engaging topic, doing good data collection, interpreting well, and discovering something that is really new and interesting. Take a chance. Pretest your journal ideas first as conference presentations or posters. This will provide feedback, lead to discussions, and give you an idea of what is clear and what is confusing. Ask colleagues for a friendly but critical review. Have fun!

References

Akaka, M., & Schau, H. (2024), "Telling stories with textual and visual analyses," in R. Belk, & C. Otnes (Eds.), *Handbook of qualitative research methods in marketing* (2nd ed., pp. 460–470). Cheltenham, UK: Edward Elgar.

Askegaard, S., & Linnet, J. (2011), "Towards an epistemology of consumer culture theory: Phenomenology and the context of context," *Marketing Theory*, 11(4), 381–404.

Belk, R., Fischer, E., & Kozinets, R. (2013), *Qualitative consumer and marketing research*. Los Angeles, Sage.

Belk, R. (2019), "On Standing Out and Fitting in," *Journal of Global Fashion Marketing*, 10(3), 203–227.

Belk, R., Humayun, M., & Brouard, M. (2022), "Money, possessions, and ownership in the metaverse: NFTs, cryptocurrencies, Web3, and wild markets," *Journal of Business Research*, 153, 198–205.

Belk, R., Sherry, J., & Wallendorf, M. (1988), "A naturalistic inquiry into buyer and seller behavior at a swap meet," *Journal of Consumer Research*, 14(4), 449–470.

Cavusoglu, L., & Belk, R. (2023a), "Face value," *16-Minute Video*. https://vimeo.com/813448542, Password: ACR2023LR.

Cavusoglu, L., & Belk, R. (2023b), "Face value, trailer," *45-Second Video*. https://vimeo.com/847072711?share=copy.

Cavusoglu, L., & Belk, R. (2024), "How to make a collaborative videography using phygital affordances to study sensitive topics," *Qualitative Market Research*, 27(3), 413–432.

Chatman, S. (1978), "Story and discourse: Narrative structure in fiction and film, Ithaca, NY: Cornell University Press," in R. Belk, & C. Otnes (Eds.), *Handbook of qualitative research methods in marketing* (2nd ed.). Cheltenham, UK: Edward Elgar.

Denny, R. (2024), "Pushing the boundaries of ethnographic practice in business," in R. Belk, & C. Otnes, (Eds.), *Handbook of qualitative research methods in marketing* (2nd ed., pp. 398–408). Cheltenham, UK: Edward Elgar.

Denny, R., & Sunderland, P. (Eds.). (2014), *Handbook of anthropology in business*. Walnut Creeek, CA: Left Coast Press.

Joy, A., & Sherry, J. (2003), "Speaking of art as embodied imagination: A multi-sensory approach to understanding aesthetic experience," *Journal of Consumer Research*, 30(2), 259–283.

Östberg, J., & Hartman, B. (2024), "Researching the cultural role of brands," in R. Belk, & C. Otnes (Eds.), *Handbook of qualitative research methods in marketing* (2nd ed., pp. 344–355). Cheltenham, UK: Edward Elgar.

Pink, S. (2001), *Visual ethnography*. London: Sage.

Price, L., Moisio, R., & Arnould, E. (2024), "Making context matter: Selecting research contexts for theoretical insights and substantive importance," in R. Belk, & C. Otnes (Eds.), *Handbook of qualitative research methods in marketing* (2nd ed., pp. 12–24). Cheltenham, UK: Edward Elgar.

Saint-Exupéry, A. (1943/2000), *The little prince* (R. Howard, trans.). San Diego, CA: Harcourt.

Van Maanen, J. (1988), *Tales from the field: On writing ethnography*. Chicago: University of Chicago Press.

West, N. (1933), *Miss Lonelyhearts*. South Australia: University of Adelaide, *eBooks@Adelaide*.

Yang, H., & Chattopadhyay, A. (2024), "Understanding consumer behavior in the metaverse," in R. Belk, & C. Otnes (Eds.), *Handbook of qualitative research methods in marketing* (2nd ed., pp. 139–149). Cheltenham, UK: Edward Elgar.

Concluding Remarks

The arts manager conducts research to know the answer to a management or marketing problem, while the academic researcher conducts research to contribute to the advancement of knowledge. Both will use the methodology best suited to fulfill their objective. In the case of the arts manager, the challenge is to determine the method that will provide the most useful information for decision-making. In the case of the academic researcher, the appropriate method must be selected to be able to answer the research question in a way that makes a contribution to our understanding of the research topic. The basis for being published by a scientific journal is the contribution to science. If this contribution is minimal, the journal will not accept the manuscript. The leitmotif is therefore in all cases "contribution, contribution, contribution."

To be able to advance knowledge in a field, one must first ensure that one is familiar with the literature on the subject. A good literature review not only allows one to become familiar with a subject, but it also helps identify different avenues of research, define a problem, and identify a gap in knowledge. It is this search for the gap that will lead to identifying a research question that has the potential to lead to an interesting contribution. It is then that the researcher will choose the most appropriate method to collect and analyze the data necessary for this research. In some cases, these will be qualitative methods; in others, they will be quantitative methods. There are a variety of methodological approaches to data collection and analysis.

The emphasis must be on selecting the right research method for the research question. Finally, the researcher must find a way to effectively and persuasively communicate their research question, methodology, findings, and contribution to an academic or managerial audience. All of this must be done in accordance with rigorous research ethics.

This book has sought to provide a thorough yet accessible framework to enable the novice or experienced researcher to take a systematic approach to developing an interesting and relevant research question, understanding the existing knowledge on the topic, identifying the appropriate research method, and conducting the research in a rigorous and ethical manner. In doing so, this book provides real-world, empirical, and theoretical insights into how to navigate the complexities of research methods in a creative context.

INDEX

Note: Page numbers in *italics* indicate a figure and page numbers in **bold** indicate a table on the corresponding page. Page numbers followed by "n" with numbers refer to notes.

For Product Safety Concerns and Information please contact our EU representative GPSR@taylorandfrancis.com Taylor & Francis Verlag GmbH, Kaufingerstraße 24, 80331 München, Germany